Coastal and Deep Sea Navigation for Yachtsmen

BY

C. A. LUND

Lieut-Commander, R.N. (Retd.) author of "The Handling of Motor Craft."

GLASGOW

BROWN, SON & FERGUSON, LIMITED

52-58 DARNLEY STREET

Third Edition - 1949

Printed and made in Great Britain by
BROWN, SON & FERGUSON, LTD., GLASGOW, S.1.

FOREWORD

BY

ADMIRAL A. V. CAMPBELL.

"These men see the works of the Lord and His wonders in the deep."

TO the yacht owner who is his own "master," this book should be of the greatest assistance. It may be that he has not had the advantage of a course of navigation, but has delved into many works seeking for knowledge.

Here he will find it briefly and concisely set out, and with the aid of a sextant and an *Inman's Nautical Tables* should be able to fathom the problem of position finding at sea in any but foggy or cloudy weather.

In narrow waters, in soundings or in sight of land, the problem presents minor difficulties only. In the open sea, dependent on the assistance of the heavenly bodies, an elementary knowledge of trigonometry must be brought to bear and put to good use.

Safety demands that the navigator should be confident of his ship's position and no opportunity of checking it should be missed.

In reading this book I began to wonder if I had not forgotten more than I had ever learnt, seeing that in the higher ranks of the Service so much is done for one by juniors.

CONTENTS

SECTION I—COASTAL NAVIGATION.

SECTION II.—DEEP SEA NAVIGATION.

CONTENTS

SECTION I.—COASTAL NAVIGATION.

CHAPTER I.

Compass Course Correction.

THE mariner's compass consists, essentially, of a copper bowl filled with water and alcohol (to prevent freezing) in which floats a card, on the under side of which are fixed two or more magnets. The card is graduated in degrees and points and quarter points, with the North at the end of the magnets which seek the North. North and South are 0 degrees, East and West are 90 degrees, therefore S.W. would be S. 45° W. and N.N.E. would be N. 22½° E., etc. In small vessels the course is usually steered by compass points, but for the purpose of the chartwork we shall use degrees only.

On the fore side of the compass bowl is a black line called the Lubber's Point, and this marks the ship's compass course. A line drawn through the Lubber's Point and the centre of the compass card is parallel to a line drawn from the bow of the ship to the stern, so that if the N. point of the compass is 50° to the right of the Lubber's Line the compass course is N. 50° W.

A line drawn from the geographical North Pole of the earth to the South Pole at right angles to the equator is called a True Meridian, but a magnetic compass will

1

not point along this because the magnetic poles of the earth are situated at considerable distances from the geographical poles.

The lines of magnetic force between the magnetic poles of the earth are called Magnetic Meridians, and the angle between the magnetic and true meridians at any place is called the "Variation." It is called easterly variation if the northern part of the magnetic meridian is to the east of the true meridian, and westerly if to the west.

As the magnetic poles are gradually moving, so the variation at any place changes from year to year, and the amount by which it does so is shown on the chart at the compass rose.

Now if a compass is kept away from all iron and steel the line through the N. and S. points (which we will call the "compass meridian") will lie along the magnetic meridian at the place where the compass is, but the presence of iron or steel in the vicinity of the compass will cause the compass card to be deviated from this direction. In fact, a steel vessel is actually a large magnet.

The angle between the magnetic meridian and the "compass meridian" is called the "Deviation," and is named easterly if the N. end of the compass is deflected to the east of the magnetic meridian, and westerly if to the west.

The deviation varies with the changes of the ship's course, and a Deviation Table (see Deviation Table at front of book) is drawn up for each vessel showing the deviation on various compass courses as will be explained later.

The "Compass Error" is the sum or difference of the deviation and the variation. If both are easterly or both are westerly they are added. If one is easterly and the other westerly they are subtracted and the error is called by the name of the larger. Thus, deviation 2° E., variation 14° W., compass error 12° W. Or deviation 3° E., variation 12° E., compass error 15° E.

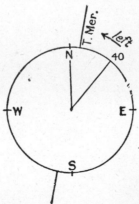

Now if the ship's compass course is N. 40° E., deviation

3° E., variation 14° W., and we wish to find the true course (that is the angle between the true meridian and the fore and aft line of the ship) we first find the compass error. It is 11° W.

Now face the direction of the compass course and if the error is *westerly* apply it to the *left*. This means that we must subtract 11 from 40, and the true course will be N. 29° E.

Again, suppose the compass course is S. 70° E., deviation 2° W., variation 12° E., the compass error will be 10° E. If the error is *easterly* apply it to the *right*.

Therefore 10 must be subtracted from 70 and the true course will be S. 60° E.

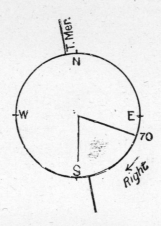

Again, suppose the compass course is N. 80° W., deviation 3° W., variation 14° W. The compass error is 17° W. This must be applied to the left, which means

we must add 17 thus making the true course N. 97° W.
As this is more than 90° we must subtract it from 180°
thus making the true course S. 83° W.

This is the method we use to find the true course,
which we can lay off on the chart when we know the
compass course that the helmsman is steering.

Now if we know that the *true* course from one place
to another (as ascertained from the chart) is N. 50° W.,
the deviation being 3° E., and variation 15° W., and we
wish to find what course to steer by compass, we reverse
the foregoing rule. That is, easterly error must be
allowed to the left, and westerly to the right.

In this case the error is 12° W., and must be allowed
to the right. Face N. 50° W. and allowing 12° to the
right will mean that we must subtract 12 from 50, making
the compass course N. 38° W.

To sum up:—

When bringing compass to true, E. right, W. left.
When bringing true to compass, E. left, W. right.

One of the methods by which the deviation of a
yacht's compass may be found is by "swinging ship."

The vessel is moored and steadied on each of the eight
principal points of the compass in succession, and the
compass bearing of a distant object is taken on each
course or direction of the vessel's head. The mean of
all these bearings gives the *magnetic* bearing of the object,
and if the differences between this magnetic bearing
and each of the compass bearings are taken the deviation
on each course is obtained.

Example.

Ship's head by compass	Compass bearing of distant object	Deviation as ascertained
N.	N. 53° E.	1° E.
N.E.	N. 56° E.	2° W.
E.	N. 58° E.	4° W.
S.E.	N. 59° E.	5° W.
S.	N. 55° E.	1° W.
S.W.	N. 52° E.	2° E.
W.	N. 50° E.	4° E.
N.W.	N. 49° E.	5° E.

$$8) \overline{432°}$$
$$\overline{54°}$$

Magnetic bearing of object N. 54° E.

Taking the first deviation, the magnetic bearing of the object is N. 54° E., so if the direction of it by the compass is to be N. 53° E. it means that the N. of the compass card must have been deviated to the east.

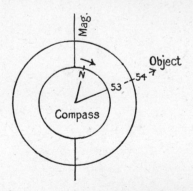

In the foregoing example all the bearings are to the eastward of north, but if it happens that some are

east and some are west, we take the sum of the easterly
ones and the sum of the westerly ones. Then subtract
the lesser sum from the greater and divide by 8, giving
as before the magnetic bearing of the object which is
named E. or W. according to which is the greater.

Example.

Ship's head by compass	Compass bearing	Deviation
N.	S. 13° W.	18° W.
N.E.	S. 21° W.	26° W.
E.	S. 23° W.	28° W.
S.E.	S. 1° E.	4° W.
S.	S. 32° E.	27° E.
S.W.	S. 39° E.	34° E.
W.	S. 25° E.	20° E.
N.W.	S. 3° E.	2° W.

Easterly bearings total S. 100° E.
Westerly bearings total S.   57° W.

$$8\overline{)\ 43°}$$
$$5°$$

Magnetic bearing is S. 5° E.

The following figures will show how the deviation is
ascertained:—   MN   means Magnetic North.
                                      CN   means Compass North.

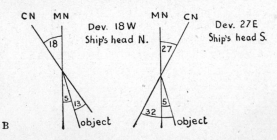

B

CHAPTER II.

ON FIXING POSITION.

THE charts most often in use are those on the Mercator Projection. It is not necessary at present to go into the principle on which this depends as it is described in the deep sea navigation section.

Look at a chart of the English Channel. The vertical lines are called meridians of longitude, and it will be noticed that they are equidistant from each other, and also parallel. Their direction is true north and south. The scale at the top and bottom is the longitude scale, and it will be seen that it is marked in degrees and minutes, there being 60 minutes (abbreviated to 60') to 1 degree. Longitude is measured E. or W. from the meridian of Greenwich.

The horizontal lines are called parallels of latitude, and the scale at each side is the latitude scale. There are 60' in 1 degree and also 1 minute of latitude=1 nautical mile (=6080 feet or 10 cables).

It will be noticed, however, that 10 miles at the bottom of the latitude scale is not the same length as 10 miles at the top of the scale. The reason for this is that in representing a sphere on a plane surface distortion occurs. Therefore distance between two places should always be measured on the part of the latitude scale abreast of the two places.

The latitude scale and the longitude scale are never the same except at the equator, so distances must always be measured on the latitude scale.

The compass roses show both true and magnetic directions, but it is more convenient to work always from the true or outer circle because the variation changes from year to year. On the English Channel chart it will be seen that the variation is decreasing 9′ annually, so if the chart in use was about 13 years old the magnetic circle would be in error by about 2°.

True courses or bearings may be written either in a similar way to the magnetic or from 0° to 360°. For instance, S. 55° E. (true) may be expressed as 125° and N. 35° E. (true) as 035°.

To lay off a course from one place to another, say from the Eddystone to St. Anthony Point, lay the parallel ruler with one edge on the two places and then slide it across until the same edge is on the centre of the compass rose. If the nearest true compass rose is some distance from the course, rule a line between the two places so that it cuts a meridian and read the course with a protractor.

Thus the true course from the Eddystone to St. Anthony is S. 86° W. The distance measured with the dividers on the latitude scale is 28 miles.

———

There are various methods of fixing a vessel's position when in sight of land, and the first to be considered will be the method of Cross Bearings.

Two conspicuous objects on shore are picked out, and

by holding a pencil upright on the edge of the compass furthest from you, look across the compass at one of the objects, moving the pencil until the object, the pencil, and the centre of the compass are in line, and note the bearing under the pencil.

(This is a rough method, but if the compass is not fitted with sight vanes or an "azimuth mirror" it will answer the purpose. Small liquid prismatic compasses for holding in the hand are made for use in yachts, and are better than the steering compass for taking bearings.)

Now take a bearing of the second object, and after correcting them both for deviation (if any) and variation as ascertained from the chart, lay them off on the chart.

Let us take an example.

Assume the compass course of the ship to be N. 20° E. at the time of taking the bearings, and the compass bearing of Wolf Light N. 29° W., and of the Lizard Light N. 71° E. With compass course N. 20° E. we find that the deviation is $4\frac{1}{2}$° W. (see Deviation Table at front of book). The variation from the chart, corrected to 1933, is $13\frac{1}{2}$° W., therefore the true bearings are N. 47° W. and N. 53° E. respectively. See chart.

Lay the parallel ruler on the true (or outer) circle of the compass rose along N. 47° W. (313°), and slide it across until one edge is on the Wolf Light, and draw a line from the light. Do the same with the Lizard bearing, and the point where the two bearings cut is the position of the ship, namely Lat. 49° 47′ N., Long. 5° 34′ W.

The objects should be chosen so that the angle between

the bearings is as near 90° as possible, because with a very acute or very obtuse angle between them a small error in taking the bearings will produce a large error in position on the chart.

If it is possible the bearing of a third object should be taken, and as it will be extremely improbable that all three bearings will meet at one point, the ship will be within the "cocked hat" or triangle formed by the bearings.

Another method of fixing the position of the ship, and a very accurate one, but one which is not always possible, is by getting two objects on shore in transit (or in line with each other), and then taking a bearing of a third object as nearly at right angles to the line of transit as possible.

For instance, if we see that Triagoz Light is in line with Sept Iles Light, and Ile de Bas Light bears 188°, our position must be Lat. 48° 52′ N., Long. 4° W.   See chart.

In cases where the speed of the vessel is known with a fair degree of accuracy (by using a patent log, common log, or revolutions of engine if under power) another method of fixing the position can be used, in which only one fixed object is needed for taking bearings.   This method is called a "Running Fix."

(*Note.*—Buoys should not be used for taking bearings to fix position as they are liable to shift.)

Let us suppose that at 9·15 a.m. we are in an estimated position 50° 5′ N., 4° 44′ W., and our true course is 095° The speed of the vessel is 8 knots.   See chart.

At 10·30 a.m. we take a bearing of Eddystone Light and find it is 050°.

At 11·30 a.m. we take another bearing of it and find it is 335°.   We can find the position of the vessel at 11·30 as follows:

From the estimated position lay off the course, and then lay off the 10·30 bearing of the light.   From where this bearing cuts the course lay off along the course the distance sailed between 10·30 and 11·30, namely 8 miles. Through this last point draw a line parallel to the first bearing.   Now lay off the second bearing, and the point at which it cuts the *first bearing transferred* is the position of the vessel at 11·30 a.m., namely 50° 6′ N., 4° 12′ W.

We know that at 10·30 we were somewhere on the first bearing line, though not necessarily at *D*, and at 11·30 we must be somewhere on the transferred bearing, assuming that we did travel 8 miles in the interval. Also, at 11·30 we know that we must be somewhere on the second bearing, therefore we must be at *B*, the point where the two lines cut.

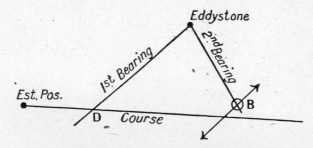

It is advisable to mark the transferred position line or bearing with an arrow at each end.

In some cases the ship's position can be ascertained by a modification of a true running fix.

For instance, suppose the ship is to the southward of the Bishop Light, sailing S. 80° E. (true) at 8 knots, and at 11 p.m. the Bishop Light bore N. 20° W. (true) and at 1 a.m. the Wolf Light bore N. 25° E. (true). We can find position of the ship at 1 a.m. as follows. See chart.

Lay off the bearing of the Bishop Light (S. 20° E. true *from* the light). The ship is therefore somewhere on this line at 11 p.m.

Lay off the course S. 80° E. (true) from the Bishop Light, and measure off along it a distance of 16 miles, and draw a line through this point parallel to the first bearing. At 1 a.m. the ship is therefore somewhere on this line.

Now lay off the bearing of the Wolf Rock Light, and where it cuts the transferred bearing of the Bishop Light is the position of the ship at 1 a.m., namely 49° 43′ N., 5° 58′ W.

In many cases the effects of a tidal stream have to be allowed for, but these will be dealt with later.

———

Another very useful method of fixing the position of the vessel is that known as a "Four Point Bearing." It is really a simplified running fix.

The time when a fixed object bears 4 points on the bow (45° from the ship's course) is taken, and then again when the object is on the beam (90° from the course). If we know the speed of the vessel, then the distance run between the two bearings is the distance off the object when it is abeam.

For instance, suppose the course steered is east, and the time when a shore object bears N.E. is 10 a.m., and the time when it bears N. is 10.30 a.m., then if the speed is estimated to be 5 knots the distance off the object when abeam will be $2\frac{1}{2}$ miles.

The importance of this method is that no lines need be drawn on a chart.

It could also be done by taking the time of the beam bearing, and also the time when 4 points abaft the beam. The distance run equals the distance off when it was abeam.

The same method may be adopted with angles other than 45° and 90°. For instance, the times when the object bore 2 points on the bow and then 4 points on the bow could be taken, and the distance run between the bearings would be equal to the distance off at the second bearing. This is called "Doubling the angle on the bow."

One disadvantage of the "Four Point Bearing" is that we do not know how far off the shore the ship will be until the object comes abeam, and if this happens to be a headland with outlying rocks the ship may run into danger.

A better method in this case is to use angles of 35° and 67° instead of 45° and 90°.

We note the log reading when the headland bears 35° on the bow and again when it bears 67° on the bow. Then the distance run between the bearings is the same as the distance that the ship will be off the headland when it comes abeam, if she continues on the same course. As we know the beam distance before we get there, we have plenty of time to alter course if necessary to clear the danger.

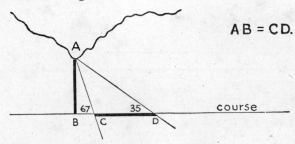

AB = CD.

Another method which can sometimes be used is by taking the bearing of a light at the moment when it is seen to "dip" below the horizon, and then finding one's distance off either by tables or by calculation.

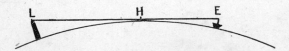

Suppose L is a lighthouse, the height of the lantern being 75 feet above the sea. E is the observer in the ship 7 feet above the sea, and H is the point on the earth's surface where the horizon would be when the light was just observed to dip.

The distance EL is $EH+LH$.

In the Nautical Tables under the heading of "Distance of Sea Horizon," and with a height of eye of 7 feet, the distance of horizon will be found to be 3·04 miles This is EH.

Now imagine the observer to be *L* (75 feet above the sea). His horizon would be 9·94 miles away. Therefore the distance of the light when it dips is 12·98 miles (say 13 miles).

It might happen that no tables were available, and in that case the distance could be calculated by formula.

The distance of the horizon in miles is $\sqrt{\frac{4}{3}\,h'}$

In this case $L\,H = \sqrt{\frac{4}{3} \times 75} = \sqrt{100} = 10$ miles.

$$E\,H = \sqrt{\frac{4}{3} \times 7} = \text{roughly} \quad \sqrt{9}$$
$$= 3 \text{ miles.}$$

Therefore the total distance is 13 miles.

Thus if we know our bearing from the light and its distance we know our position.

The heights of most lighthouses are given on the chart in feet above the level of high water spring tides, so in order to be accurate an allowance has sometimes to be made for the height of the tide.

(*Note.*—The visibility of lights as shown on the chart is always for a height of eye of 15 feet.)

CHAPTER III.

PATENT LOG AND CHART READING.

THE speed of a yacht may be ascertained in various ways, the accuracy of each depending on the type of vessel.

For instance, in a fast motor cruiser the "Patent Log" will probably be the most accurate. It should be borne in mind that the length of log line most suitable varies with different vessels, and the correct length should be ascertained by trial. Also in nearly every log there is a certain amount of error, and when possible the percentage error should be found by testing the log over a measured distance. As a log registers the speed through the water and not over land, the error should be found by traversing the measured distance both with and against the tidal stream so as to counteract its effect.

Let us take an example. At the top of the Admiralty chart for Southampton Water will be seen a measured distance of 6079 feet. There are 6080 feet in a nautical mile so we can call this a measured mile. The course along this measured mile is S. $54\frac{1}{2}°$ E. or N. $54\frac{1}{2}°$ W. (true).

At the south-eastern end, the beginning of the mile is marked by a pecked line passing through two beacons with a triangle on each. The north-western end is marked by two similar beacons.

Suppose we are proceeding to sea and wish to find

the error of the log. We stream the log some time before reaching the N.W. end of the mile, and setting our course S. $54\frac{1}{2}°$ E. (true) as nearly as possible, at the instant when the two beacons are in line we take the reading of the log. Suppose it is 2 miles and 3 tenths, and the time is 10h. 5m. When the other two beacons come in line the log shows 3 miles and 4 tenths and the tide is 10h. 11m. 30s. Assume that this run has been done against the tide. The actual speed was 6079 feet in 6m. 30s. or 9·23 knots.

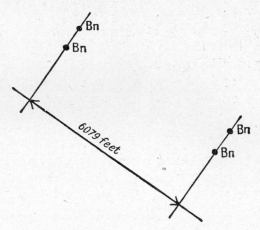

Now after turning round we steam back along the course and take the readings as before, this time with the tide.

    1st beacons 10h. 14m. 0s.   log 4·1 miles.
    2nd beacons 10h. 19m. 30s.   log 4·9 miles.

The speed in this case was 6079 feet in 5m. 30s. which is 10·91 knots. The mean of these speeds is 10·07 knots, and this was the speed of the vessel *over the ground*. The patent log gave a speed of $1\cdot1+0\cdot8$ ($=1\cdot9$) miles in 12 minutes, which is $9\cdot5$ knots. So the speed of the ship as shown by the patent log is too small by $0\cdot57$ knot in $9\cdot5$ knots, and this is an error of 6 per cent. underlogging.

This figure may be written inside the patent log box for further reference.

It is important to keep the revolutions of the engine as constant as possible while the test is being carried out.

Note.—When hauling in the rotator of the log, in order to take the turns out of the line as the rotator is hauled in, the other end should be veered over the stern and the line coiled down starting with the rotator end.

A patent log is not usually accurate at speeds below 5 knots. For lower speeds the old common log is the more accurate, although somewhat cumbersome. It is quite simple to make, and after various speeds have been found by its use the navigator will in time be able to estimate his speed without its aid.

The "log ship" consists of a triangular piece of wood with sides 8 inches and base 6 inches, with a strip of lead on the base to make it float apex upwards in the water. Three lines or bridles are attached to the corners, one of them being fixed to a peg which loosely fits in a hole in the apex of the log ship.

The bridles are spliced on to a length of cod line, and about 15 fathoms from the log ship a piece of white rag is tucked into the line. Now wet the line and stretch it, and mark off equal lengths of 47 feet 3 inches with small pieces of leather, and procure a suitable reel to revolve on a spindle.

To use it, put the peg in the hole, drop the log over the stern, and when the white rag passes overboard take the time. Count each piece of leather as it goes out, and

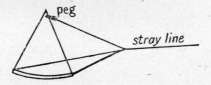

when 28 seconds have elapsed hold on to the log line. The jerk will pull the peg out of the hole, and the log ship may be hauled in lying flat on the water.

The number of pieces of leather which have passed over the stern indicate the number of knots of speed—the number of nautical miles per hour.

An even simpler method, and yet quite an accurate one, is called the "Dutchman's Log." A piece of wood is thrown overboard in the bows, and the time taken with a stop watch. When it reaches the stern the time is taken again. Suppose the length of the ship is L feet and the time taken is T seconds, then the speed of the the ship in knots $= \dfrac{6 \times L}{10 \times T}$. The calculation is a very simple one, and although the method may seem crude it works very well in practice, even in small yachts.

The question of speed estimation in sailing craft with winds of variable force is a difficult one, but by first learning to judge speed by eye with the use of the common log, the navigator should be able to form a very fair estimate of the average speed of his vessel without any external aids.

Chart Symbols.

The principal symbols used on new Admiralty charts are given below, but a complete list of them may be obtained at any of the Admiralty Chart Agents.

Description of sea bottom.—Adjectives, small letters; nouns, capital letters. Thus, blk. S., means black sand; cG means coarse gravel.

E.D.	Existence doubtful
P.D.	Position doubtful
P.A.	Position approximate
	} Current
	Flood stream
	Ebb stream
	3 hours after high water (H.W.)
	Anchorage for large vessels
	Anchorage for small vessels
	Wreck submerged
	Wreck exposed at L.W.
	2 hours after low water (L.W.)
2 K N	Ebb at 2 knots.

Numbers on sea give depth below datum (usually low water ordinary spring tides—L.W.O.S.). Soundings are generally in fathoms, but the units are always given in the title.

$\frac{\circ}{60}$ means no bottom at 60 fathoms.

Heights on land are in feet above H.W.O.S.

<u>2</u>   means that a bank dries 2 *feet* above datum or
          L.W.O.S.

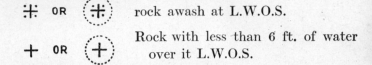

⌗ OR (⌗)   rock awash at L.W.O.S.

+ OR (+)   Rock with less than 6 ft. of water
                    over it L.W.O.S.

≋   overfalls or tide rips.

- - - - - - - - - - - -   4 fathom line.

- - - - - - - - - - - - - -   5   ,,   ,,

— — — — — —   6   ,,   ,,

— - — - — - — - —   10   .,   ,,

— - - — - - — - - —   20   ,,   ,,

The pecked line dividing the white part of the chart
from the grey is the low water mark of ordinary spring
tides, and the black line separating the grey from the
land is the high water mark.

The system of buoyage round the coasts of the United
Kingdom is uniform.

When entering harbour or going in the direction of the
flood stream the right hand side is called the *starboard
hand*. It must therefore be remembered that when
leaving harbour or going in the direction of the ebb
stream the port hand will be on the right.

Starboard hand buoys are always conical in shape,
and are painted either black or black and white chequers.
They are sometimes surmounted by a black cone or
diamond. If a starboard hand buoy has a light it
will be white, and may show 1, 3 or 5 flashes.

Port hand buoys are always can shaped (flat topped) and are painted either red or red and white chequers. They are sometimes surmounted by a red can or a red "T". If a port hand buoy has a light it will be red showing any number of flashes up to 4, or white showing 2, 4 or 6 flashes.

Where there is a bank in the middle of a channel so that a navigable channel runs on each side of it, each end of the bank is marked by a Middle Ground buoy. These are always spherical and have red and white horizontal bands on them if the main channel is to the right or if both channels are of equal importance. If the main channel is to the left they have black and white horizontal bands.

Middle ground buoys may also have topmarks as follows:—

    (a) Main channel to right:—
           Outer end, a red can.
           Inner end, a red "T".

    (b) Main channel to left:—
           Outer end, a black cone.
           Inner end, a black diamond.

    (c) Channels of equal importance:—
           Outer end, a red sphere.
           Inner end, a red +.

NOTE.—The colours and top marks as described above may not always be found, as the system was only brought into force in 1947, and it will take a long time to repaint all the buoys. The shapes of the buoys remain unaltered.

C

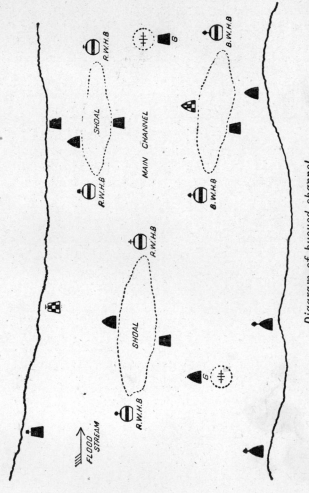

Diagram of buoyed channel.

Buoys marking wrecks are always painted green, with the word WRECK painted on the side in white. Those which are to be left on the starboard side of the ship when going in the direction of the flood stream are conical and show groups of three green flashes. Port hand wreck marking buoys are can shaped, and show groups of two green flashes, and those which may be left on either side show one green flash.

In addition to the above, there are various other types of buoys such as mid-channel marks, isolated danger marks, landfall marks, telegraph buoys and watch buoys (for light vessels).

The above shows an estuary with the open sea on the left.

The actual position of each buoy on a chart is shown by a small circle on the centre of the waterline.

The lights shown by lighthouses, light vessels and lighted buoys are of various kinds, and in addition to their characteristics being shown on the large scale charts, they are given in the Admiralty List of Lights and in Brown's and Reed's Nautical Almanacs.

A *flashing light* is one in which the period of light is less than the period of darkness, and is marked Fl.

A *quick flashing light* shows more than 60 flashes per minute and is marked Qk. Fl.

An *interrupted quick flashing light* is the same as a quick flashing one, except that there is a total eclipse at regular intervals. It is marked Int. Qk. Fl.

An occulting light is one where the period of light is longer than the period of darkness, and is marked Occ.

A group flashing light is one which gives two or more flashes of light followed by a period of darkness.

For instance, a light which is marked Gp. Fl. (2) ev. 10 sec. means that the group consists of 2 flashes, and from the beginning of one group to the beginning of the next group is 10 seconds.

A group occulting light is one which gives a steady light with a group of two or more sudden eclipses.

For instance, a light marked (U) Gp. Occ. (2) ev. 8 sec. means that it is unwatched, and shows a steady light broken at intervals by 2 "flashes of darkness". From the first of one group of 2 flashes to the first of the next group of 2 flashes is 8 seconds.

A stop watch is a very useful instrument when identifying lights.

A fixed (steady light) is marked F.

An alternating light is one which changes its colour.

―――――

When approaching an unknown coast or entering an unfamiliar harbour, care should be taken to keep to all directions given on the chart or in the Sailing Directions with regard to avoiding dangers. The two principal methods are by "Leading Marks" and "Clearing Marks".

When entering the river shown in the sketch, the beacon *A* is kept in line with the church tower *B* as long as the line is drawn full. When the beacon *C* comes in line with the other beacon *D* the course is altered so as to keep these two beacons in line.

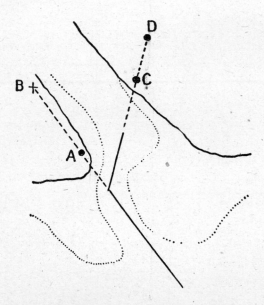

This illustrates the use of leading marks.

The line should never be followed where it is shown pecked. Leading marks are not as reliable when they are close together as when they are far apart.

Clearing marks are used to enable the ship to keep clear of a danger on one side. Let us suppose that a ship is making for *D* from the southward and there is a dangerous rock at *C*. As long as we keep the church tower at *D* open of the headland *A* we shall keep clear

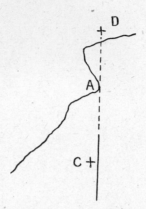

of the rock. If the church tower disappears behind the headland it will not be open, and the ship is in danger.

___

When a vessel is sailing along a coast with outlying dangers and high cliffs it is possible to estimate the distance off shore by the method known as the "Danger Angle".

Suppose the rock B is $\frac{1}{2}$ mile from the lighthouse A which, according to the chart, is 200 feet high, and we wish to keep $\frac{1}{2}$ mile to seaward of the rock—that is when passing the rock we wish to be at C.

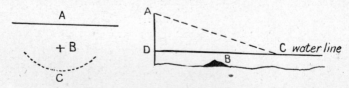

$A\,D$ is 200 ft., $D\,C$ is 1 mile, so in order to keep $D\,C$ equal to 1 mile we must keep the angle $A\,C\,D$ constant.

This may be done by means of a sextant, but a very useful little instrument has been invented by a Commodore of the Royal Cruising Club and can easily be made.

Take a cardboard tube about 2 inches in diameter and 15 inches long. Cut out a disc of cardboard to fit the tube, and in it cut a slit. Across the slit fix five thin wires each $\frac{1}{4}$ inch apart, and then stick the disc in one end of the tube.

At the other end of the tube fix a disc with a pinhole in the centre as an eyepiece.

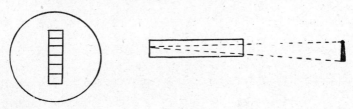

Now look through the pinhole at the lighthouse and tilt the tube until the waterline is on one wire and notice which wire is nearest to the top of the lighthouse; in other words, how many spaces the lighthouse covers.

Then the distance off in cables (10 cables=1 nautical mile)

$$= \frac{\text{Height of object in feet}}{\text{Number of spaces filled} \times 10}$$

The principle of it is that the length of the tube is 60 times the space between two wires, and if the lighthouse fills one space your distance from it must be 60 times its height.

————

To use this instrument in the previous problem—the

height $= 200$ ft., the distance off is to be 10 cables ($= 1$ mile)

therefore 10 cables $= \dfrac{200 \text{ ft.}}{\text{No. of spaces} \times 10}$

No. of spaces $= \dfrac{200}{100} = 2.$

Then as long as the lighthouse does not occupy *more* than 2 spaces we must be at least a mile from it.

When finding the distance off a cliff the waterline should be as nearly as possible vertically under the top edge.   If the waterline is considerably nearer the observer than the higher object the angle observed will be too great and the ship will be estimated to be nearer than she actually is.   However this is an error on the right side.

CHAPTER IV.

TIDES AND TIDAL STREAMS.

THE rise and fall of the tide is caused by the attraction of the sun and moon, but the whole process is very complicated and will not be dealt with except to state that the greatest effect is caused by the moon, and that when the moon and the sun are on the same side of the earth (new moon) and on opposite sides of the earth (full moon) the tides rise highest and fall lowest, and are called Spring Tides. When the moon and the sun are at right angles to each other (1st quarter and last quarter) the tides do not rise so high and do not fall so low, and are called Neap Tides.

It should be noticed that the highest tides do not occur exactly at full and new moon but usually from $1\frac{1}{2}$ to 2 days later.

The Range of any tide is the difference in height between the high and low water of that particular tide.

The Rise of a tide is the difference in height between the high water and the datum or level to which chart soundings are reduced.

The chart datum is the average lowest level to which the tides fall and is usually that of low water ordinary spring tides (L.W.O.S.). In the *Admiralty Tide Tables* the heights of the tide at high water and low water are the heights in feet above this datum.

Let us take the case of a tide of which the height of high water is 20 feet and the height of low water is 4 feet, assuming in this case that the chart datum is the level of L.W.O.S.

When the datum is the same as L.W.O.S. the spring rise and the spring range are the same. The level of the datum is given in the title of a chart, but for practical purposes it may be considered to be L.W.O.S.

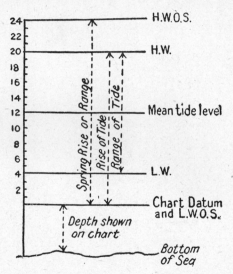

The mean tide level is half way between the high water and low water of any tide, so in this case as the low water of a spring tide is 12 feet below the mean level, the high water of a spring tide will be 12 feet above mean level.

The time of high water at any place may be found from the information given on the chart by means of the

H.W.F. & C. This means High Water Full and Change, and is the time of high water on full moon and new moon days. Finding the time of high water from the H.W.F. & C. is a very approximate method, but is useful if no tide tables are available.

Note.—The *H.W.F. & C. for Dover is* 11 24 and is a very useful one to remember as Dover is the standard port used for finding the directions of tidal streams.

The tidal information under the title on the Southampton Water chart states that the H.W.F. & C. for Southampton is Xh. 55m. (and XIIh. 57m.). This means that the time of high water on the day of full moon is 10h. 55m. after midnight, and 10h. 55m. after mid-day on the day of new moon.

The second time 12·57 is the time of the second high water, which occurs at many places on the South Coast due to the tidal stream flowing round both ends of the Isle of Wight. After the first high water the level of the tide slightly falls and then begins to rise again until the second high water. It then falls continually until low water.

The time of high water is roughly 50 minutes later each day, so if we know the date of new or full moon, and we have a chart giving the H.W.F. & C., we can find the approximate time of high water on any day.

The rate at which the tide rises or falls is not constant for every hour, and an approximate method of finding the height of the tide at any time between high and low water is the "Twelfths Rule."

In the first hour the tide rises $\frac{1}{12}$ of the range, in the

2nd hour $\dfrac{2}{12}$ of the range, 3rd hour $\dfrac{3}{12}$, 4th hour $\dfrac{3}{12}$, 5th hour $\dfrac{2}{12}$, and in the last hour $\dfrac{1}{12}$.

It may be remembered thus 1, 2, 3, 3, 2, 1 *twelfths*.

Example.—Find the height of tide at 1·30 p.m. at Cowes on January 11, 1933 (the date of full moon). H.W.F. & C. at Cowes is 11·36. The height of H.W. springs is 11½ feet above the datum, and assuming this to be L.W.O.S. the range of the tide is 11½ ft.

In 2 hours the tide will have fallen $\left(\dfrac{1}{12}+\dfrac{2}{12}\right)\times 11\frac{1}{2}=$ 3 feet approximately, so the height of the tide will be 8½ ft. above L.W.O.S. To find the depth of water we add 8½ ft. to the sounding shown on the chart at the place required.

The height of the tide very often differs considerably from the predicted height owing to weather conditions, so it is impossible to rely on them except to the nearest foot.

Let us take another example. Find the depth of water at 2·30 p.m. on January 20, 1933, in St. Ives Bay, where the depth shown on the chart is 5 fathoms.

In most tide tables, such as in *Brown's Nautical Almanac*, a table of tidal constants is given for a large number of places, and if the constant for any place is added to or subtracted from the time of high water at Dover the time of high water at the place is obtained.

The time constant for St. Ives is given as +5·47, and as H.W. at Dover on January 20 is 4·49 a.m. the time of H.W. at St. Ives must be 10·36 a.m. We want to find the height of tide 4 hours after high water. By referring to the table of phases of the moon for that month it was last quarter on the 19th, so it must be a neap tide, and the neap rise for St. Ives is given in the Almanac as $17\frac{1}{4}$ feet, and the spring rise is $23\frac{1}{4}$ feet. By drawing a rough figure to illustrate this we find that the range of the neap tide must be $11\frac{1}{4}$ feet. In 4 hours the tide falls $\frac{9}{12}$ of the range=$\frac{9}{12}$ of $11\frac{1}{4}$=about $8\frac{1}{2}$ feet, therefore the height of tide above L.W.O.S. is $17\frac{1}{4}-8\frac{1}{2}$= about 9 feet. The depth of water at that place must be 9 feet+5 fathoms=39 feet.

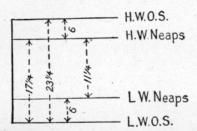

The H.W.F. & C. and the spring and neap rise are given for a large number of ports in *Brown's Nautical Almanac*. The time of the H.W.F. & C. is local mean time (L.M.T.), so if the port is considerably east or west of Greenwich a correction for longitude must be made. It is 4 minutes of time for every degree, and to find the G.M.T. (Greenwich Mean Time) we subtract it if we are east of Greenwich, and add it if we are west. A rhyme will make it easier to remember.

"Longitude west, Greenwich time best.
Longitude east, Greenwich time least."

For instance, the L.M.T. of H.W.F. & C. at Cork is
4·53. The longitude of Cork from the chart is 8° W.,
so the longitude correction is $4 \times 8 = 32$ minutes to add,
and the G.M.T. of high water at Cork on a full or new
moon day is 5·25 a.m. or p.m. respectively.

In coasting it is more important to know the direction
and rate of the tidal stream than the time of high water,
except when entering harbour or crossing a shoal.

It should be noted that a tidal stream is not the same
as a current. The latter is a movement of a body of
water in an almost constant direction (such as the Gulf
Stream), whereas a tidal stream is variable, changing
its direction and its rate with the ebb and flow of the
tide.

The arrows shown on charts show the rate and direction
of the tidal streams in different places. An arrow thus
shows the direction of the flood tide (*F*lood—
*F*eathers) 2 hours after low water in the locality, and
its rate is 3 knots. An arrow thus shows the
direction of the ebb tide 3 hours after high water, and
its rate is 2 knots.

If the speed of a tidal stream is given as 3 to 4 knots,
and it is in the same direction as the ship's course, it is
always better when approaching land to assume that
it is going at 4 knots, because the estimated speed of the
ship (over land) will put her ahead of where she will
actually be, and the error will be on the safe side.

If the tidal stream is against the ship when she is
heading towards the land, it is better to assume that the
tide is going slower, which means that your estimated

speed towards the land is greater than is actually the
case, and you will be really further from the land than
you thought.

If the ship's course is at an angle to the direction of
the tidal stream the ship's actual course over land (called
the course made good) and her actual speed over land
must be ascertained by drawing a diagram.

Suppose a ship to be sailing eastwards, and the tide
setting southwards, the ship will actually be carried in
a south-easterly direction. To take an example: a
ship's true course is east and her speed is 8 knots. The
tide sets south at 3 knots. Find the course made good
and the speed made good. Draw *A B* east and make it
8 convenient units in length, to represent the course

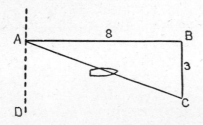

steered and the speed. Draw *BC* south, and make it 3
units long, to represent the direction and rate of the
tidal stream. Then the ship actually moves along *A C*
although her bows have been heading parallel to *A B* all
the time. The angle between *A C* and the meridian *A D*
is the true course made good, and if we measure the
length of *A C* in the same units as we measured *A B*, we
find the speed made good over the bottom of the sea.

If this is drawn to scale, it will be found to be 8½ knots.

The tide has therefore been helping the ship.   The course made good is S. $69\frac{1}{2}°$ E.

On many charts will be found tables showing the directions of the tidal streams in different positions before and after high water at Dover, and in some cases Liverpool.

For instance, let us suppose that we are in the vicinity of the Breaksea Light Vessel (Lat. 51° 20′ N., Long. 3° 17′ W.) in the British Channel at 4 p.m. on June 16, 1933, and we wish to know in what direction the tidal stream is setting.

Near the light vessel on the chart will be seen the letter (*A*), and on referring to the table of tidal streams (shown on the chart) the directions and rates will be found at various times before and after high water at Liverpool.

TIDAL STREAMS.

Position A.

	Hours	Direction	Rate	
			Springs	Neaps
Before H.W. Liverpool.	5	96	1·4	0·8 kts.
	4	276	0·8	0·4 ,,
	3	,,	3·4	1·9 ,,
	2	,,	4·8	2·7 ,,
	1	,,	4·5	2·5 ,,
	H.W.	,,	3·5	2·0 ,,

From the tide tables we see that the times of high water at Liverpool on June 16 are 5·34 a.m. and

6·7 p.m. (As a matter of fact Liverpool and Dover times are almost identical), therefore the time in question, namely 4 p.m., is 2 hours before high water at Liverpool. The table of phases of the moon shows that it was last quarter on the 14th, therefore it will be a neap tide.

From the table we find that the tide is setting 276 at 2·7 knots.

Again, south of the Lizard the tidal stream sets in a direction N. 53° E. (true) at 5 hours before H.W. at Dover, at a rate of 4 knots.

Suppose that it is this particular time, and we wish our course made good to be S.E. (true), the speed of the ship being 8 knots. What course shall we have to steer to counteract the effect of the tide?

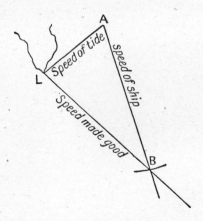

Lay off from the Lizard the course we wish to make good, namely S.E. true, and also lay off from the Lizard the direction of the tidal stream, N. 53° E. true. Choose

D

some suitable scale to represent speed (say $\frac{1}{2}$ inch=1 knot) and measure off the rate of the stream (4 knots=2 inches) on it. Now take the speed of the ship (8 knots= 4 inches) on the dividers, and with centre A make an arc to cut the course at B. Join $A\,B$.

Then the direction $A\,B$, namely S. 16° E., is the course which must be steered in order to counteract the effect of the tidal stream.

If the length of $L\,B$ is measured in the same units as $L\,A$ and $A\,B$, we shall get the "speed made good," which is the speed over the bottom of the sea. It will be found to be 7·4 knots.

It will be seen that the above figure is really half of a parallelogram, of which the speed made good is the diagonal, being the "resultant" of the speed of the ship and the speed of the tidal stream.

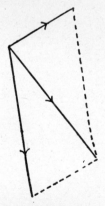

The rates of the tidal streams shown on the arrows are the maximum spring rates. The neap rates are about one-third less.

A useful book of diagrams showing the directions of tidal streams all round the British Isles at one hour intervals from high water at Dover is *The Yachtsman's Tidal Streams and Tidal Data,* published by Brown, Son & Ferguson, Ltd., and another is *Tidal Streams of the British Isles,* published by the Admiralty.

In addition to allowing for tidal streams another allowance has often to be made, especially in sailing vessels, and, in the case of strong beam winds, in all vessels. This is called leeway. The usual method of estimating leeway is to look astern and judge the angle between the fore and aft line of the ship and the wake. Naturally it can only be an approximate estimation. If the vessel is towing a log it is easier to estimate, as the angle between the log line and the fore and aft line can be seen more easily. Leeway is usually estimated in points, 1 point of the compass being $11\frac{1}{4}$ degrees. In correcting a course, the leeway is always applied in such a way as to make the corrected course further from the wind than the compass course.

For example, suppose the compass course is S. 34° W. and the wind is S.E. It is estimated that the leeway is 1 point (say 11 degrees). Then the course that the ship moves along, that is the course made good, is S. 45° W.

Whenever possible it is advisable to make the wind and tide counteract each other by "under-bowing the tide."

For instance, if a ship has to sail from *A* to *B*, northeast, the wind is N.E. and the tide is setting N., it will be better to sail on the port tack than on the starboard tack, because the leeway will tend to set the ship towards the east, but the tide will set her towards the north, and consequently they will to a great extent neutralise each other. In a power-driven vessel the course would in any case have to be set more towards the east to allow for the tidal stream.

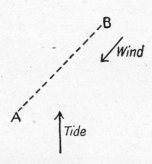

When a vessel is coasting it is often possible to find the rate and direction of the tidal stream even when they are not shown on the chart.

Suppose the vessel is in a position where St. Mary's Light bears 008° and the Bishop Light bears 310° at 10 p.m. She is sailing S. 74° E. by compass at 10 knots.

At 12·30 a.m. the Wolf Light bears 316° and the Lizard Light bears 053°. Find the observed position of the ship at 12·30 a.m. and hence the set and drift of the tide experienced since 10 p.m.

The deviation is 5° E. and the variation for 1933 was $13\frac{1}{2}$° W., so we first plot the ship's position at 10 p.m. and then lay off the true course S. $82\frac{1}{2}$° E. and measure off 25 miles along it, this being the distance run between 10 p.m. and 12·30 a.m. This gives the D.R. position at 12·30 a.m., 49° 45′ N., 5° 41′ W.

We now plot the second pair of cross bearings, and find the actual position of the ship to be 49° 47′ N., 5° 34′ W. It is obvious that the tide has set the ship from the D R position A to the observed position B, namely a distance of 5 miles in 2½ hours, therefore the tidal stream was running at 2 knots in a direction 069°. The direction of A to B is called the set, and the distance from A to B is called the drift.

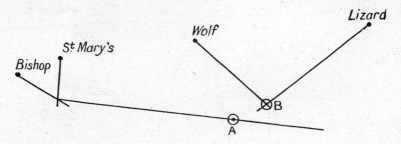

When the method of the "Running Fix" was explained in Chapter II. no allowance for tidal stream was made, and the course laid off on the chart was the course steered.

In the majority of cases when a vessel is coasting, the tidal stream will be setting either against or with the vessel and will have no appreciable effect on the course, although the speed made good will of course be affected.

But suppose we are trying to make St. Ives from the westward, and wish to find our position by means of a running fix using the Seven Stones Light. The tide sets between the islands and the mainland, and will therefore have an effect on the course made good.

Let us assume that at 9·30 p.m. the estimated position

of the ship is 50° 8' N., 6° 11½' W., the true course being N. 75° E., and speed 8 knots.

At 9·30 p.m. the Seven Stones Light bears 133° and at 10·15 p.m. it bears 208°. From the tidal diagram or from the Sailing Directions we find that between 9·30 and 10·15 the tide sets south at 2 knots. See chart.

From the estimated position at 9·30 lay off the true course, and from the Seven Stones lay off the first bearing. Measure 6 miles along the course from the point where the first bearing cuts it from A to B, and then the distance that the tide would set the ship in three-quarters of an hour, namely 1½ miles from B to C, in a southerly direction.

Through this point C draw the transferred bearing, and the position at which this transferred bearing cuts the

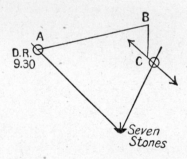

second bearing is the position of the ship at 10.15 p.m., namely 50° 7½' N., 6° 1' W.

The course made good is therefore along the direction A C.

When coasting it is advisable to fix the position of the ship as frequently as possible, so that in the event of thick weather coming on a good D.R. position will be available.

In a fog, if the vessel is near high cliffs, the approximate distance off may be found by using the siren, fog horn or whistle, and noting the length of time which elapses between the sounding of the horn and the echo.

Then the distance off in cables = number of seconds in the interval minus $\frac{1}{10}$ of the interval.

For instance, suppose the interval which elapses is 12 seconds, then the distance off is $12 - \frac{12}{10} = 10 \cdot 8$ cables, or just over a mile.

It is impossible to emphasise too strongly the importance of using the lead line when making land or entering unknown harbours.

The hand lead should weigh about 10 lbs. and the line should be $1\frac{1}{8}$ inch in size (circumference), and 25 fathoms in length. The line is marked as follows.

2 fathoms	-	-	2 strips of leather.
3 ,,	-	-	3 strips of leather.
5 ,,	-	-	white linen.
7 ,,	-	-	red bunting.
10 ,,	-	-	leather with a hole in it.
13 ,,	-	-	blue serge.
15 ,,	-	-	white linen.
17 ,,	-	-	red bunting.
20 ,,	-	-	piece of cord with 2 knots.

1, 4, 6, 8, 9, 11, 12, 14, 16, 18, and 19 fathoms have no marks, and are called "deeps."

The reason for using linen, bunting and serge is that they can be distinguished at night by touch.

It is a good plan in shallow draught vessels to make a mark at 1 fathom, although it is not orthodox.

The lead is always hove on the weather side. When heaving on the starboard side hold the coil in the left hand, and with sufficient scope to clear the water, swing the lead backwards and forwards until it has a good momentum. Then swing it completely round in a circle three times and let go as it swings forward.

By the time the lead has reached the bottom the vessel will be over it and the line will be up and down. In any case, gather in the slack of the line until the weight of the lead can just be felt.

The use of the lead line in a fog should never be omitted because by its means the approximate position of the vessel may often be determined. The cavity in the bottom of the lead should be "armed" with Russian tallow, so that particles of the sea bottom will stick to it, and the nature of these may be compared with the markings on the chart.

Suppose the vessel is in estimated position 49° 47½' N., 3° 4' W. at 10 a.m., and her true course made good (after allowing for tidal stream and leeway) is S. 33° W. and her speed is 6 knots. A cast of the lead is taken every quarter of an hour and each sounding is corrected according to the state of the tide so as to obtain the depth at L.W.O.S.

The following soundings (after correction) are taken:—

10·00 a.m.	37	fathoms
10·15	37	„

10·30 a.m.	38 fathoms	
10·45	38	,,
11·00	39	,,
11·15	35	,,
11·30	45	,,
11·45	56	,,
12·00	49	,, Sand and shells
12·15	50	,,

Now take a sheet of tracing paper, rule a meridian on it, and several more lines parallel to the meridian

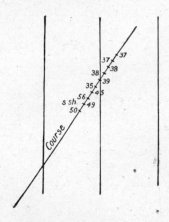

about an inch apart. Lay off the true course made good, S. 33° W., and mark off equal distances along it, representing the distance the vessel travels in each quarter of an hour, namely 1½ miles. Opposite each mark write the corrected sounding, and then lay the paper on the chart with the first mark somewhere near the D.R. position. Keeping the ruled lines parallel to one of the meridians on the chart, move the paper

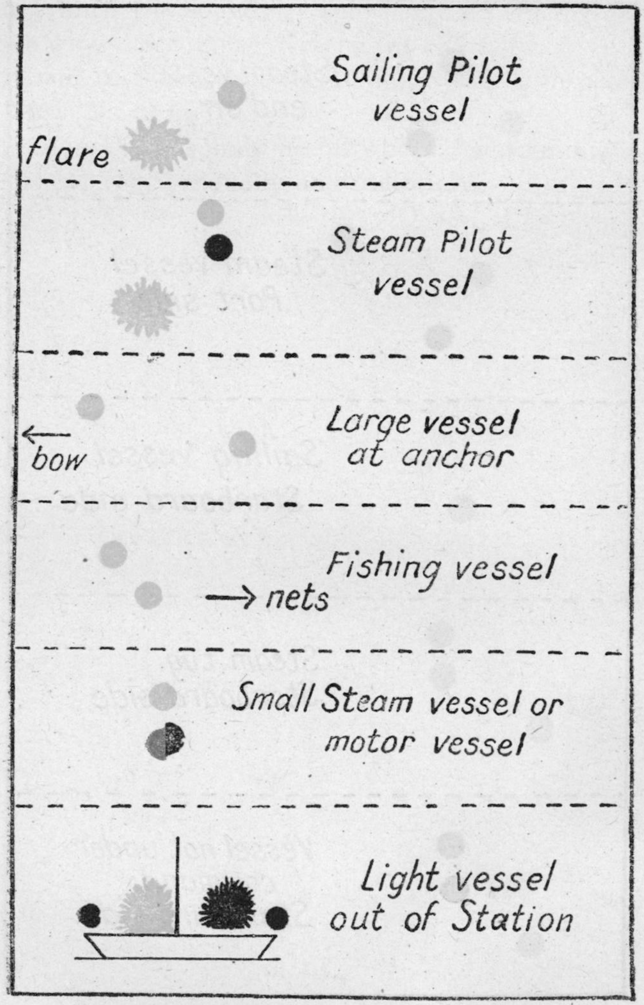

Sailing Pilot vessel

flare

Steam Pilot vessel

← bow Large vessel at anchor

Fishing vessel

→ nets

Small Steam vessel or motor vessel

Light vessel out of Station

CHAPTER V.

RULE OF THE ROAD.

ALL persons navigating yachts or any other type of vessel should make it their business to study in detail the "Regulations for Preventing Collisions at Sea." They will be found in *Brown's Nautical Almanac*.

The lights displayed by all classes of vessels are described minutely, and also the sound signals to be used in fog and by power driven vessels in sight of each other.

The steering and sailing rules should certainly be committed to memory so that instant action can be taken to avoid collision.

A few of the more common lights are given here.

It is a common fallacy for small motor cruisers to carry a combined lantern showing white, green and red lights, but no authority for this will be found in the Regulations, as Article 7, section 2, expressly states that the white light shall be carried *above* the side-lights or the combined lantern.

When meeting another vessel in daylight it is comparatively easy to see if there is any risk of collision, but at night this is a different matter. Whenever a vessel's light or lights are sighted a bearing should *always* be taken with the compass, and if the bearing remains

47

the same the vessels will collide.   If the bearing draws ahead or astern the vessels will clear each other.

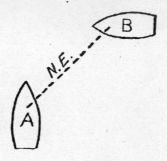

For instance, *A* and *B* are two mechanically driven vessels, and the bearing of *B* from *A* is N.E.   If the bearing of *B* becomes N.N.E., *B* will pass ahead of *A*, and if it becomes E.N.E., *A* will pass ahead of *B*.

But if the bearing remains N.E., *A* must alter speed or course so as to pass astern of *B*, while *B* *must keep straight on*.

If *A* is a sailing vessel, *B* must alter course to pass round her stern.

Usually it is not necessary to alter course very much, but it is advisable to find out what course the other vessel is steering.   In the daytime this can fairly easily be seen.

As it will be seen in Article 2 (*d*) and (*e*), the side-lights are visible from right ahead to 2 points abaft the beam— that is 10 points for each light—and this fact enables us to judge the other vessel's course.

For example, suppose you are heading N. and you see

a green side-light bearing N.E. Then the other vessel must be steering between S.W. and E.S.E.

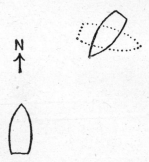

In order to visualise this in actual practice, we reverse the bearing (which gives S.W.), and if it is a green light add 10 points anti-clockwise (giving E.S.E.). If it is a red light add 10 points clockwise.

Again, suppose you are steering N.W., and 4 points on your starboard bow you see a red light.

The bearing will be N. and the reversed bearing is S. Add 10 points clockwise—W.N.W. Therefore the other vessel is heading between S. and W.N.W.

Actually when she is heading S. you will see both lights, and when heading W.N.W. the red light will just be disappearing.

The course which a sailing vessel is steering can often be known within smaller limits than in the case of a steam vessel, because she cannot sail closer to the wind than 4 points, and in the case of a square-rigged vessel 6 points.

For instance, suppose the wind is E. and you see a sailing vessel's green light bearing W.N.W. She cannot

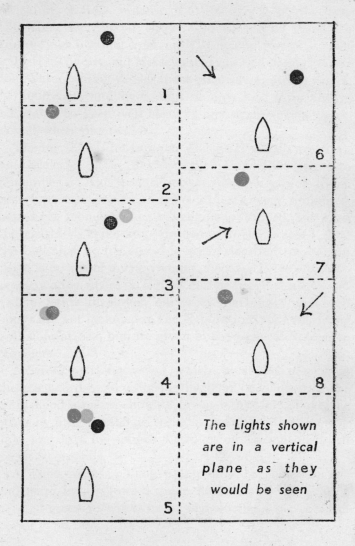

The Lights shown
are in a vertical
plane as they
would be seen

A wreck-marking vessel to be passed on the port hand shows 2 green lights, or 2 green balls, vertically above each other, and sounds 2 strokes on the bell in a fog.

A wreck-marking buoy to be passed on the port hand is can shaped and green, and shows 2 green flashes.

A wreck-marking vessel which may be passed on either side shows 2 green lights, or balls, on one yardarm, and 2 on the other.

In addition to the lights for vessels given in the Regulations, it should be noted that a yacht sailing from a foreign port, on arrival at a British port, must report to the Customs and get her clearance, and must show a white light at night under the bowsprit until she is cleared.

As a summary of this chapter a few illustrations of various cases of "Rule of the Road" are given, and the reader should try to visualise the course the other ship is steering in each case.

In examples 1 to 5 it is to be assumed that the reader is in a power-driven vessel, and in 6, 7, and 8 in a sailing vessel. The wind is shown by the arrow.

1. Keep clear.
2. Keep clear.
3. Keep clear.
4. Keep course and speed.
5. Alter course to starboard.
6. Keep clear.
7. Keep clear.
8. Keep course and speed.

SECTION II.—DEEP SEA NAVIGATION.

CHAPTER I.

THE SEXTANT.

In order to fix the position of a vessel at sea by means of observations of celestial bodies we find the altitude of the body by means of a sextant.

It will be assumed that the reader either possesses a sextant or at least can obtain the use of one.

It consists of a metal frame supporting two mirrors. One of these is fixed, and is called the "Horizon Glass." The upper part of it is plain glass, and the lower part silvered. The other mirror is fixed to the "Arm," and is called the "Index Glass."

The arm revolves about a pivot, and on one end of it is a small scale called the "Vernier," which slides along the bigger scale which is called the "Arc." It may be clamped to the arc by the "Clamping Screw" underneath, and may be moved very gradually by means of the "Tangent Screw." Some sextants are fitted with a micrometer screw instead of a vernier.

It will be seen that the arc is graduated in degrees and tens of minutes, and the vernier in units of minutes and tens of seconds.

Owing to the light from the body observed being twice reflected, the angle between the mirrors is only half the angle shown on the arc. Thus when the mirrors make an angle of 45° with each other the index on the vernier reads 90°.

Before a sextant is used for taking observations it should be tested for errors as follows.

(1) *Error of Perpendicularity.*—This occurs if the index glass is not perpendicular to the plane of the instrument. Set the arm about a third of the way along the arc, and holding the sextant horizontally with the index glass towards you, look into it at the reflection of the arc. If the reflection of the arc and the actual arc just on the right hand edge of the mirror are not in the same straight line the index glass is not perpendicular, and in this case the screw on the back of the glass must be adjusted.

(2) *Side Error.*—This occurs if the horizon glass is not perpendicular to the plane of the instrument.

Set the index (the arrow on the right of the vernier scale) at zero, hold the sextant horizontally, look through the collar at the horizon. If the horizon seen in the

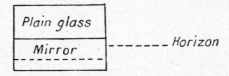

silvered part of the horizon glass is above or below the actual horizon to the right of the mirror the horizon glass is not perpendicular, and the screw at the bottom centre of the glass must be adjusted until the two parts of the horizon are in line. If in harbour any horizontal line will do, but it should be 2 or 3 miles distant.

(3) *Index Error.*—When the index is at zero the two mirrors should be parallel with each other.

Set the index at zero, focus the inverting telescope and screw it into the collar. Put a coloured shade in front of each mirror and look at the sun.

Now move the tangent screw until two suns appear, and adjust it until their inner edges just touch. Read the angle, and suppose it is 34' 20" on the arc. (That is the index is to the left of the zero.)

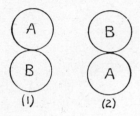

Now turn the tangent screw until the reflection of the sun (*B*), which was at the bottom, crosses over the actual sun (*A*) and just touches it at the top as in (2).

The reading of the index will now be off the arc (to the right at zero).

```
  36'  40"  off
  34'  20"  on      Suppose it is 36' 40". Subtract the
  ─────────          lesser from the greater and divide by 2,
2) 2'  20"           and the result is the index error.
  ─────────
   1'  10"  +
```

When the index error (usually written I.E.) is off the arc it means that every angle read on the sextant is too small by that amount, and it is always to be added.

Instead of using the mirror shades, an eyepiece shade may be put on the telescope.

If the motion of the vessel is too violent to enable the index error to be taken in this way it may be roughly found as follows.

Set the index at zero, and holding the sextant vertically, look through the collar at the horizon. If there is no index error the horizon in the plain glass should be exactly in line with the horizon as seen in the mirror. If it is not, turn the tangent screw until the two horizons are in line, and read the angle on the scale.

The index error is not usually taken out unless it is very great, because in doing so one is liable to put in side error again. The amount of it is noted down and applied to the observed altitude of the celestial body.

----

(4) Another error which is sometimes found, and which may be caused by the telescope being knocked or the collar bent, is called "Collimation Error." It is due to the optical axis of the telescope not being parallel with the plane of the instrument.

(*Note.*—The telescope may be moved bodily up and down by means of the screw under the collar, but this does not cause collimation error, as the telescope remains parallel.)

Put in the inverting telescope and focus it, turning it round until two of the wires are parallel with the plane of the instrument.

Pick out two stars about 90° apart and bring them

into exact contact with each other by looking at the right hand star and moving the arm slowly round, keeping the star in the mirror until it coincides with the left hand star. Tilt the sextant slightly keeping them in contact on the bottom wire.

Now tilt the sextant upwards to bring them on the upper wire, and they should still appear in contact. If they do not remain in contact there is collimation error, and it must be corrected by tilting the telescope by means of the two screws on the collar, *A* and *B*.

To tilt the eyepiece down, ease screw *A* and tighten *B*.

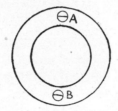

To tilt the eyepiece up, ease B and tighten *A*, but be careful *always* to ease one before tightening the other.

There are various other errors, but they can only be corrected by an optician. In fact, the most important error of all is the index error, and this should be ascertained before every sight.

When using the sextant to take angles between terrestrial objects and star sights, the telescope with the large object glass and low magnification should be used.

For sun sights the long telescope with either the eyepiece with two cross wires or the one with four should be used. When the sun is somewhat blurred the lower magnification eyepiece (4 cross wires) should be inserted.

It is advisable to focus the telescope on the horizon and scratch lines round the eyepiece tubes so as to save the trouble of focussing on future occasions.

Now when we take the altitude of a celestial body at sea we are finding the angle between the body and the horizon at the observer's eye. The horizon which we see is called the visible horizon, and as the observer's eye is above the surface of the sea the direction of this visible horizon is not horizontal, or in other words is not at right angles to the zenith.

In the figure, O is the observer's eye and $V H$ is the direction of the visible horizon. Z is the observer's

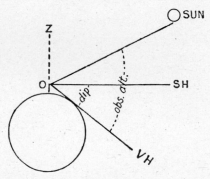

zenith, and $O S H$ is the sensible horizon, at right angles to $O Z$.

The angle between the sensible and visible horizons is the dip, and this depends on the height of the observer's eye above sea level. This is the first correction to be subtracted from the observed altitude (marked obs. alt.).

As rays of light pass through space they travel in straight lines, but on reaching the earth's atmosphere they become bent or refracted, so that an observer at

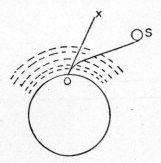

O would see the sun, which is actually at *S*, apparently at *X*. When the sun is vertically overhead the refraction is zero, and when low down on the horizon it is at a maximum. The correction for refraction has to be subtracted from the observed altitude.

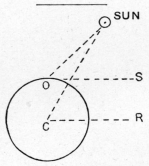

As the observer is on the surface of the earth instead of being at the centre, another correction called parallax has to be applied. If the observer were at the centre of the earth his horizon would be in a direction *C R*, which

is called the rational horizon, and is parallel to the sensible horizon. It is obvious that the angle sun $O\,S$ is not equal to the angle sun $C\,R$, and the angle O sun C is the Parallax, and is added.

It will be noticed that in this figure the altitude is the angle of the *centre* of the sun above the horizon, whereas in practice we usually reflect the bottom edge of the sun down to the horizon. This is called the "sun's lower limb." Therefore, to find the true altitude of the centre of the sun above the rational horizon we must apply a correction for the half diameter of the sun, called the "sun's semi-diameter," and this varies inversely as the sun's distance from the earth.

There is no need to apply all these corrections separately because in the Nautical Tables the "Sun's Total Correction in Altitude" will be found, in which by taking the height of eye and the observed altitude of the sun's lower limb (marked ☉) we can find the correction to *add* to the observed altitude, but care must be taken to apply the small correction at the bottom of the page allowing for the *variation* in the sun's semi-diameter.

Let us take an example.

Find the true altitude of the sun's centre on July 1, if the observed ☉ was 47° and the height of eye was 12 feet. The index error of the sextant was 2′ 30″ +

Obs. alt.	47°	0′	For H.E. 12 ft. and obs. alt.
I.E. (+)		2·5	47° the correction is 11·8′ on
	47°	2·5′	July 1. The correction for
Sun's corr. (+)		11·6′	variation in semidiameter is
			−0·2′
True alt. -	47°	14·1′	Total correction 11·6′.

When an altitude of the sun is taken, the index is set at zero, and after the suitable shades are adjusted in front of the index glass (and also the horizon glass if there is much glare on the sea), the sun is reflected down until its lower limb just touches the horizon. Now screw in the inverted telescope and very slightly swing the sextant so that the sun describes an arc *below* the horizon. Adjust the tangent screw until the edge of the sun just touches the horizon at the top of its swing. At this instant take the time by a watch, the error of which on G.M.T. is known.

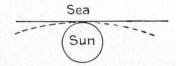

Sea

Sun

The method of finding the altitude of the sun at noon is slightly different.

Ten minutes before noon (ship apparent time) reflect the sun down to the horizon, and keep looking at it every minute, adjusting the tangent screw *while the altitude is getting greater*. Then (about noon) the sun will not appear to move for a few minutes, but as soon as it is seen to be going down read the angle on the arc, as this is the maximum altitude that the sun has reached, and, provided the ship is not moving rapidly on a northerly or southerly course, is the meridian altitude.

The method of finding the latitude of the ship from this will be described in the next chapter.

imagined that there is a great sphere at an infinite distance around the earth called the Celestial Sphere. On this are situated the celestial bodies including the sun, stars, etc.

On the celestial sphere in line with the poles of the earth are the celestial poles p and p_1.

The celestial equator $e\,q$ is parallel to the earth's equator, and the celestial meridians such as $p\,m\,p_1$ are parallel to the earth's meridians.

Due to the rotation of the earth, the sun and other bodies on the celestial sphere appear to travel round the earth from east to west, and due to the yearly rotation of the earth round its orbit the sun appears to move round the celestial sphere along a path called the Ecliptic $t\,s$ from west to east. The ecliptic cuts the Celestial Equator at two points, and the point where the sun is crossing the celestial equator from south to north is called the First Point of Aries (γ).

Thus it will be seen that the sun is sometimes south of the equator, sometimes on it, and sometimes north of it, and the angular distance between it and the equator is called the Declination. The declination therefore is the arc of a celestial meridian between a celestial object and the celestial equator. It is measured in degrees, and corresponds to latitude on the earth.

The declination of the sun for every two hours on each day is given in the *Nautical Almanac*, and the declination of each of the principal stars is given for each month at the beginning of each month in the *Nautical Almanac*.

The maximum declination of the sun is 23° 27' N. and S. on June 22 and December 22 respectively.

In the figure the maximum northerly declination of the sun is represented by the arc *s q*.

The zenith is the point on the celestial sphere immediately above the observer's head. Thus the zenith of an observer at *O* on the earth is at *Z*.

As the celestial sphere makes one revolution in 24 hours the *celestial* equator is divided into hours, minutes and seconds. The hour angle of a celestial object is the angle at the celestial pole between the observer's celestial meridian and the meridian passing through the centre of the object, measured in a *westerly* direction. It can also be expressed as the arc of the celestial equator between the two meridians. For instance, in the figure, *p* is the celestial pole, *P* is the N. pole of the earth, *X* is a star, *Z* is an observer.

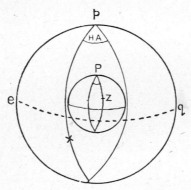

Then the angle at *p* is the hour angle. In this case it will be seen that the observer is in N. latitude and the star's declination is South.

As the earth is also a sphere, we can also say that the hour angle is the angle at *P* between the observer's meridian and the meridian passing through the point on the earth where the star would be immediately overhead.

Another method of illustrating hour angle is by a figure on the plane of the equator.

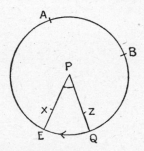

Imagine you are above the celestial pole *P*, and are looking downwards to the equator *A E Q*. Then *Z* is the zenith of the ship, *X* is the star (which may be either North or South of the equator), *P Q* is the ship's celestial meridian, and *P E* the celestial meridian passing through the star. Then the angle at *P* is the hour angle of the star; or it may be expressed as the arc of the equator *E Q*. In this case the hour angle is about 3 hours. If the star's meridian passed through *A* the hour angle would be 12 hours, if through *B* it would be 18 hours, and if the star was on the meridian of the ship its hour angle would be 0 or 24 hours.

As explained before, the sun travels round the celestial sphere yearly along the ecliptic, and its hour angle is measured in exactly the same way as that of the star in the above example, but as its apparent motion is not uniform a clock could not be constructed to keep time with it.   For this reason an imaginary sun is used, called the Mean Sun, and this is supposed to move at a constant rate, and the time by it is called Mean Time.

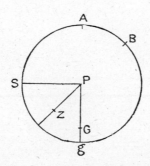

In the figure, on the plane of the equator G is the position of Greenwich and Pg the meridian of Greenwich. (It is immaterial whether the figure represents the celestial sphere or the earth.   In the former case G would be the zenith of Greenwich.)   S. is the mean sun, in this case on the equator, but it may be N. or S. of it.   The hour angle is 6 hours (west from Greenwich) and the Greenwich Mean Time (or G.M.T.) is 6 p.m. or as it is called in astronomical time 18 hours.

When the mean sun is at A the G.M.T. is 0 hours, and when on the meridian of Greenwich it is 12 hours or noon.

Suppose there is a ship at Z, in longitude 45° west of Greenwich.   The sun has passed the meridian of the ship three hours ago, so the time at the ship (or the ship mean time, S.M.T.) is 3 p.m. or 15 hours.   When the sun is at B the S.M.T. will be 0 or 24 hours.

As the sun goes round the earth (apparently) once

(360°) in 24 hours, 1 degree of longitude represents 4 minutes of time, so 45° would be 3 hours. This is called the longitude in time. In the Nautical Tables the conversion of angular longitude into time will be found at the top of the Haversine Table.

If we are given G.M.T. and the longitude of the ship, we can find the S.M.T. by a simple rule:—

"Longitude East, Greenwich Time Least.
Longitude West, Greenwich Time Best."

Examples.—(1) G.M.T. 10 hours 15 minutes, longitude of ship 50° 14′ E. Find S.M.T.

	G.M.T.	10h 15m 0s
Long. E. (in time)		3h 20m 56s (add)
	S.M.T.	13h 35m 56s

(2) S.M.T. 18h 40m 20s on January 14, ship in Longitude 125° W. Find G.M.T.

	S.M.T.	18h 40m 20s	14th Jan.
Long. W. (in time)		8h 20m 0s	(add)
	G.M.T.	27h 0m 20s	

As this is more than 24 hours it will be on the next day, so the *G.M.T. will be 3h 0m 20s on January 15.*

It was stated that the actual sun (called the Apparent or True Sun) does not move at a uniform rate, therefore the time as shown by a sundial will not be the same as the time on a chronometer showing mean time, except at certain times of the year. The difference between these two times (called apparent time and mean time) is called the Equation of Time. Since January 1, 1925, when the astronomical day began at midnight instead of noon, the equation of time has not been used, although it is still included in some Nautical Almanacs. An amount called E is tabulated instead. (E is 12 hours minus equation of time, or equation of time is 12 hours minus E.)

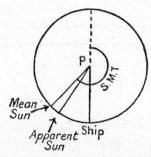

Now S.M.T.$=12$h $+$ H.A. of mean sun

$= 12$h$+$H.A. of apparent sun$+$Eq. of T.

$= 12$h$+$H.A. of apparent sun$+(12$h$-E)$

$= 24$h$+$H.A. of apparent sun$-E$.

24 hours is a whole day so may be neglected, and the simple formula becomes S.M.T.$=$H.A. of apparent sun$-E$.

To make it easy to remember it may be made to rhyme thus:—

> "Hour angle minus E
> Is equal to the S.M.T.

The values of E for every 2 hours of the day will be found in the *Nautical Almanac* for each day of the month.

Suppose we wish to find the G.M.T. when the hour

F

and by simply applying the declination from the Almanac we can find our latitude, as the figure on the plane of the meridian will show.

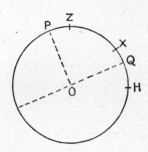

O is the observer, and *Z* is his zenith.   *H* is the rational horizon, 90° from *Z*.   *P* is the *N* celestial pole and *Q* is the celestial equator, 90° from *P*.   *X* is the sun or other heavenly body on the observer's celestial meridian.

The arc *X H* is the altitude of the body.

The arc *X Q* is the north declination of the body.

The arc *Z X* is the zenith distance.

The arc *Z Q* is the latitude (because an arc of a meridian on the celestial sphere is proportional to the arc on the earth immediately under it).

Now the latitude $Z Q = X Q + Z X$
$$= X Q + (90° - X H)$$
$$= \text{declination} + 90 - \text{altitude}.$$

This holds good when the body is *south* of the observer and the declination is *north*, and *vice versa*.   If both are north or both are south the declination will have to be subtracted.

This rule may be remembered best thus:—When the

bearing and declination of the body have the *S*ame names—*S*ubtract.

Example.—On Jan. 4, 1933, in Long. 37° 30′ W., the observed meridian altitude of the sun's lower limb (obs. mer. alt. ☉) was 41° 22·5′ south of the observer, I.E., 2′ 30″+, height of eye 20 ft.   Find the latitude.

_____

It will be seen from the formula that in order to find the latitude we must know the declination, and in order to look up this we must know the G.M.T. of the observation.   We know that the sun was on the meridian, and therefore its hour angle was 0 or 24 hours, so the S.A.T. was 12 hours.

Applying the longitude (in time) to this we get the G.A.T., which will be sufficiently close to the G.M.T. to enable us to look up E.

Now H.A.$-E=$S.M.T., so by subtracting E from 24 hours we get the S.M.T., and by applying the longitude to this we get the G.M.T.   With this we can look up the sun's declination.

The work is arranged thus:—

S.A.T.	12h	0m	0s	Jan. 4
Long. W.	2	30	0
G.A.T.	14	30	0	Jan. 4, $E-$11h 54m 58s.
H.A.	24h	0m	0s
$E-$	11	54	58
S.M.T.	12	5	2
Long. W.	2	30	0
G.M.T.	14h	35m	2s.	Jan. 4, Dec. 22° 44′ S.

stars are given in the *Nautical Almanac* for each month. It will be seen that they vary very slightly from month to month.

In exactly the same way the right ascension of the mean sun is the angular distance eastwards from the first point of Aries to the mean sun; and is written R.A.M.S.

As right ascension (on the celestial sphere) corresponds to longitude (on the earth), and declination in the same way corresponds to latitude, the position of a body on the celestial sphere can be fixed by measuring its right ascension eastwards, from the first point of Aries, and its declination north or south of the celestial equator.

Similarly if we measure the angular distance between γ and the meridian passing through the zenith of the ship it is the right ascension of the meridian (R.A.M.).

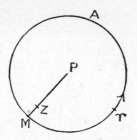

In the figure, *Z* is the zenith of the ship, *P M* is the meridian, and the arc γ *A M* is the right ascension of the meridian, namely about 18 hours in this case.

If we measure the angular distance westwards *from* the meridian of the ship *to* the first point of Aries it is called the Sidereal Time. Numerically it is the same as the R.A.M.—the only difference is the direction in which it is measured.

The sidereal time at the ship (or the R.A.M.) is found by adding a quantity called R to the ship mean time. R is tabulated in the *Nautical Almanac* instead of R.A.M.S., and it is equal to R.A.M.S. $\pm$ 12 hours. Its use was introduced at the same time and for the same reason as E is used instead of equation of time.

However the main point to remember is that *Ship Sidereal Time (or R.A.M.)=S.M.T.+R.*

Example.—At about 2 a.m. on January 7, 1933, in a ship in Long. 120° E., the chronometer showed 6h 20m 0s. Find the sidereal time at the ship.

We must first find G.M.T. As the chronometer only shows time up to 12 hours the G.M.T. may be 6h 20m or 18h 20m, so in order to find which of these it is we take the rough ship time (*R.S.T.*) and apply the longitude to it, giving rough Greenwich time or G.D.

R.S.T.	2h	0m	0s	January 7
Long. E	8	0	0	
G.D.	18h	0m	0s	January 6

Therefore the correct G.M.T. must be 18h 20m 0s on January 6. With this time look up R in the Almanac. At 18 hrs R is 7h 3m 26·5s and the difference in 2 hours is 19·7 secs, therefore using the Table of Proportional Parts 20 minutes produces a difference of 3 secs. As R is getting bigger we add the difference, and R at 18h 20m is 7h 3m 30s to the nearest second.

diameter have no effect. The star's total correction will be found in Inman's.

Obs. alt.	41° 26′	
I.E. —	2	
	41° 24·0	
* Corr.	5·8	Star corr. is always *minus*.
True alt.	41° 18·2′	

Now look up Pole Star Table I, and with sid. time 0h along the top and 13m down the side we find the first correction is —0° 59·6′.

Table II. with altitude 40° and sidereal time 0h 13m we find the second correction is +0·1′.

With Table III and January 1 the third correction is +1·0′.

Now apply these corrections to the true altitude, and the result will be the latitude of the ship.

True alt.		41° 18·2′
1st corr.	—	59·6
		40° 18·6
2nd corr.	+	0·1
3rd corr.	+	1·0
Lat. N.		40° 19·7′

A Pole Star sight should be taken in the evening or early morning when the horizon is clearly visible, although in summer time in the north it is possible to take the altitude at any time of the night.

CHAPTER IV.

TRAVERSE TABLE.

THE shortest distance between any two places on the earth's surface is along the arc of the great circle joining them.

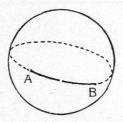

If a figure is drawn on a sphere, such as a tennis ball, with a piece of chalk, this will be obvious, but for practical purposes the use of a sphere for laying off courses would be quite impossible, so the spherical earth has to be represented on the plane surface of a chart.

It is not possible to fold a first piece of paper round a sphere so that it will touch it everywhere, so for the purpose of making charts projections are used, and the commonest is that known as the Mercator Projection.

The principle of it is as follows.

Imagine a cylinder of paper to be placed round a glass sphere on which the parallels of latitude and the meridians of longitude are marked, and so that the paper touches the sphere at the equator.

Now if a lamp be placed at the centre C the shadows of

the parallels will be projected on to the paper as shown in the figure, and it will be seen that although the

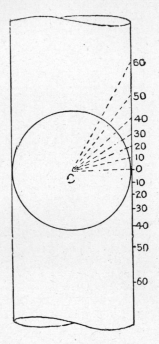

parallels of latitude are equidistant on the sphere they gradually become further apart on the paper as the latitude increases, but they will all appear as straight lines running east and west.

As the meridians of longitude around the equator are equidistant from each other so they will be equidistant on the paper and will appear as straight lines running north and south.

Considering again the spherical surface of the earth,

as one minute (1′) of latitude is equal to one nautical mile, one minute of longitude *measured along the equator* is also equal to one nautical mile, but *nowhere else*. Thus, if we measure the distance between two meridians along a parallel of latitude north or south of the equator, that distance in miles will not be equal to the number of minutes of difference of longitude between those two meridians. Owing to the convergence of the meridians towards the poles it will be less, and is called the Departure.

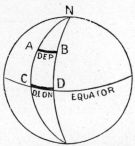

In the figure, *A* and *B* are two places on the earth, and it will be seen that the departure *A B* is less than the distance *C D* on the equator.

Departure is therefore the number of miles that a ship makes good in an easterly or westerly direction.

Now supposing a ship starts from a position in Lat. 30° N., Long. 40° W. and sails on a course N. 50° W. (true) for a distance of 35 miles we can find by means of the Traverse Table in *Inman's Nautical Tables* the amount she has altered her latitude, and the departure she has made, and hence find her new position, without drawing a line on the chart.

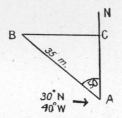

A B is the track of the ship. *N A B* is the course.

A C is the difference of latitude in miles (or minutes) between *A* and *B*.

C B is the departure in miles between *A* and *B*.

Turn up the Traverse Table in *Inman's Nautical Tables*, and with 50° as course, and 35 miles as distance we find in the Diff. Lat. column 22·5′ and in the Dep. column 26·8′.

As the lat. of *A* is 30° 0′ N. and the course was northerly, the difference of latitude must be added to the lat. of *A* giving the lat. of *B*=30° 22·5′ N.

Now the departure of 26·8′ is the number of miles between *A* and the meridian of *B* due west, and this will not be the same on the equator. To find how many miles it would be on the equator, in other words the difference of longitude, we turn up the table in Inman's called Departure into D. longitude. (This saves working out the formula D. Long.=Departure × Sec. middle Lat.) We take the latitude mid-way between that of *A* and *B* to the nearest degree, namely 30°, along the top of the page, and in the column below it opposite to departure 27 (or 26·8) we find that the difference of longitude is 31·2. By taking the exact departure 26·8 and interpolating, the difference of longitude would be 31.

Now as the vessel has sailed westwards and the longitude of *A* was 40° W. we add the difference of longitude, giving the longitude of *B* 40° 31′ W. Therefore the position of *B* is Lat. 30° 22·5′ N. and Longitude 40° 31′ W.

If the course had been southerly and easterly the difference of latitude and difference of longitude would have been subtracted.

This method is especially useful in the case of a yacht beating to windward, if the scale of the chart is too small to plot all the alterations of course.

Let us take the example of a vessel which leaves a position Lat. 50° 10′ N., Long. 18° 30′ W., and sails on the following courses for the given distances. (The courses have been corrected for deviation, variation and leeway, and are therefore true courses.)

N. 60° W., 20 miles; S. 30° W., 25 miles; N. 65° W., 26 miles; S. 20° W., 22 miles.

The work is arranged thus:—

True Course	Distance	D. Lat.		Dep.	
		N.	S.	E.	W.
N. 60° W.	20	10·0	—	—	17·3
S. 30° W.	25	—	21·7	—	12·5
N. 65° W.	26	11·0	—	—	23·6
S. 20° W.	22	—	20·7	—	7·5
		21·0	42·4 S.		60·9 W.
			21·0 N.		
			21·4 S.		

G

After entering the D. lat. and dep. we add up the N. and S. columns, and subtract the smaller from the greater, putting the sign of the greater. Also do the same with the E. and W., but in this case all the departure is westerly.

Latitude from   50° 10·0′ N.
Diff. lat.   -   21·4′ S.

Latitude to - 49° 48·6′ N.

Now find what difference of longitude corresponds to a departure of 60·9 miles in latitude 50°. By turning to the departure in D. longitude table we find that the D. long. is 94·7′ W. (by interpolating between 93·3 and 94·9). We can now find the new longitude:

Longitude from   18° 30·0′ W.
Diff. long.   -   94·7′ W.

Longitude to   20°   4·7′ W.

The position the ship has arrived at is therefore Lat. 49° 48·6′ N., Long. 20° 4·7′ W., and this position can be pricked off on the chart with accuracy, whereas it would have been almost impossible to have laid off each course and distance separately on an ocean chart.

It is important to bear in mind that the courses written down in the foregoing table are not the courses steered. Each compass course must be converted from points into degrees (if necessary), and then corrected for deviation, variation and leeway.

The Traverse Table is based on right angled triangle plane trigonometry, and saves the navigator the trouble of solving the triangle himself.

It is advisable to know the reason for using the various tables, when practicable, and the following simple explanation of the trigonometry on which the Traverse Table depends is given.

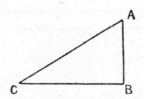

In a triangle containing a right angle at B, if the length of $A B$ (perpendicular) is divided by the length of $A C$ (the hypotenuse), the quotient is called the Sine of the angle at C. Also if the length of $C B$ (the base) is divided by the length of $A C$, the quotient is called the cosine of C. Now suppose the angle of C is 30° and $A C$ is 20 miles, and we wish to find the length of $A B$.

We know that $\dfrac{A B}{A C} =$ sine of 30°, therefore $\dfrac{A B}{20} =$ sine 30°, or $A B = 20 \times$ sine 30°.

Now look up the sine of 30° in the Table of Natural Sines in the Nautical Tables, and we find it is ·50000, therefore the length of $A B = 20 \times ·5 = 10$ miles.

Now it will be seen that $\dfrac{A B}{A C}$ in addition to being the sine of C is also the cosine of the angle A. This will be easier to understand if the triangle is turned round so

CHAPTER V.

ON FINDING THE LONGITUDE.

HAVING now dealt with methods of finding the latitude by day and by night, we will see how the longitude may be obtained. This is a more difficult business, and the knowledge of a certain amount of trigonometry must be gained before attempting a longitude problem. It will, however, be reduced to a minimum.

A spherical triangle is a triangle drawn on the surface of a sphere, and its sides are arcs of great circles, and the lengths of them are therefore measured in degrees, minutes and seconds (or in miles, as 1' on a great circle= 1 nautical mile).

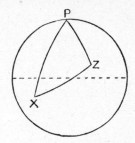

In the figure, in the spherical triangle $P X Z$, P is the N. pole, X is the geographical position of a celestial body, and Z is the position of the ship.

The dotted line represents the equator.

If the figure is made to represent the celestial sphere, instead of the earth, P will be the celestial pole, X will be the celestial body, and Z the zenith of the observer.

It will be noticed in this case that the declination of the body is south, its hour angle $Z P X$, and the latitude of the ship is north.

$P Z$ is 90°—latitude, and is called the co-latitude.

$P X$ is 90°+declination, and is called the polar distance.

ZX is the zenith distance, which is always 90°—altitude.

Let us suppose that we take the altitude of the sun, and note the G.M.T. at the same time. If we can find the S.M.T., and then take the difference between the S.M.T. and the G.M.T., we shall know the longitude of the ship.

Now the S.M.T.=the hour angle of the true sun minus E, so from the triangle we have to calculate the angle $Z P X$, which is the westerly hour angle of the sun.

The fundamental formula for solving a spherical triangle, when the three sides are known, is a somewhat lengthy one but very important. The algebraical and trigonometrical processes by which it is obtained need not be dealt with. The explanation of the terms sine and cosine have already been given when dealing with the Traverse Table, but there are two more which must now be understood.

The haversine of an angle is half the versine, and the versine is 1 —the cosine. Therefore the haversine of an angle $A = \dfrac{1 - \text{cosine } A}{2}$.

We will now work out a complete longitude sight, by the "Longitude by Chronometer" method.

On Jan. 5, 1933, about 1600 at ship, in 42° 36′ S, 47° 28′ W., by D.R. the obs. alt. ☉ was 36° 22·5′; height of eye 12 feet; G.M.T. by chronometer 19h 17m 3s (Jan. 5). Find the longitude of the ship.

The procedure is as follows. Look up the sun's declination and E with the given G.M.T. in the *Nautical Almanac*. Correct the observed altitude (by the Sun's Total Correction Table) and then find the zenith distance. Find the sun's hour angle by working out the spherical triangle formula. Subtract E from it, giving the S.M.T. Take the difference between the G.M.T. and the S.M.T. giving the longitude in time. Convert this into degrees and minutes.

It is always advisable to draw a rough figure, and if this one is drawn on a tennis ball with chalk it will be easier to understand.

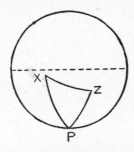

First mark the position of the ship Z in South latitude, and draw the co-latitude PZ from the South Pole. Now as the rough ship time is 16 hours (4 p.m.) the sun will be west of the ship, and its declination in January will be south, so the position of the sun will be at X, and $P X$ will be the polar distance. Draw an arc of a great circle joining Z and X, and $Z X$ will be the zenith distance. The angle at P is the hour angle.

G.M.T.　　=19h 17m 3s Jan. 5　$\left\{ \begin{array}{l} \text{Dec. S. } 22° \ 36·1' \\ E \text{ 11h 54m 25s} \end{array} \right.$

$P X = 90° - \ 22° \ 36·1' = 67° \ 23·9'$
$P Z = 90° - \ 42° \ 36' \ \ = 47° \ 24'$

Obs. alt.　　　$36° \ 22·5'$
Sun's corr.　$+$　　　$11·7$

True alt.　　　$36° \ 34·2'$
　　　　　　　$90°$

Zen dist.　　　$53° \ 25·8'$　　nat hav ·20210
　$= Z X$

$P X$　　　　　$67° \ 23·9'$
$P Z$　　　　　$47° \ 24'$

$\sim$　　　　　$19° \ 59·9'$　　nat hav　·03015

　　　　　　　　　　　　　　　　·17195 Subt.

　　　　　　　　　　log hav　　9·23540
$P X = 67° \ 23·9'$　　log cosec　0·03470
$P Z = 47° \ 24'$　　　log cosec　0·13306

　　　　　　　　　　log hav P = 9·40316 add all
　　　　　　　　　　　　　　　　　　　three.

Hour angle P = 4h 1m 36s.

H.A.　　　4h 1m 36s　add 24h to H.A. before
E −　　　11 54 25　　　subtracting E

S.M.T.　16　7　11
G.M.T.　19　17　3

Long. W.　3h 9m 52s subtract.

Convert this into arc by looking in the Haversine Table for 3h 9m at the top of the page, and next to it will be found 47° 15′. Then look down the left hand side of the page in the faint type for 52s and 13′ will be found. Add this to 47° 15′ and the result is 47° 28′ which is the longitude.

As the G.M.T. is greater than the S.M.T. the longitude is west.

It will be seen that in this case the D.R. longitude is exactly the same as the observed longitude, but this would seldom be the case in practice.

In this method of finding the longitude it will be noticed that we used the D.R. latitude in solving the spherical triangle, therefore, unless the sun was bearing due east or west, an error in the latitude would produce an error in the observed longitude. For this reason it is best, when possible, to take a longitude sight when the sun's true bearing is as nearly as possible east or west—namely on the prime vertical (a great circle passing through the observer's zenith and the east and west points).

If the latitude has been found at the previous noon by a meridian altitude of the sun, we can find our position at the time of the longitude sight provided we know the course made good and the distance run between the two sights.

By means of the Traverse Table we find the difference of latitude and then apply it to the latitude at noon.

For instance, taking the foregoing example, we will suppose that the latitude at noon by a meridian altitude of the sun was 43° 14′ S., and between noon and the time of taking the longitude sight the ship sailed N. 28° E. (true) for a distance of 43 miles.

With course 28° and distance 43 miles the difference of latitude is 38′ North, and as the observed latitude at noon was 43° 14′ S. the latitude at the time of the longitude sight is 42° 36′ S., and hence the position of the ship at 1600 is Lat. 42° 36′ S., Long. 47° 28′ W.

Similarly if the longitude sight had been an A.M. one the departure and hence the difference of longitude between the two sights could be taken and applied to the observed longitude, thus giving the longitude at noon, which in conjunction with the meridian altitude sight would give the position of the ship at noon.

CHAPTER VI.

POSITION LINES.

THE position of a ship at sea may be found by a method of "celestial cross bearings" and by a "celestial running fix." It is called the Marcq St. Hilaire method.

If we take the altitude of a celestial body and subtract it from 90° we obtain the zenith distance, or the distance from the ship to the geographical position of the body. If at the same time we take the true bearing of the body, we know our bearing and distance from it, and consequently we know the position of the ship, provided we know and can plot on a chart the geographical position of the body. Usually the zenith distance is a matter of hundreds or thousands of miles, and hence the positions of the ship and the body cannot be plotted on a chart.

However, we generally know more or less the position of the ship on the earth—in other words, we have a dead reckoning position—and if we calculate by means of the spherical triangle our zenith distance, and also find our true zenith distance by taking an altitude, by taking the difference between these we can ascertain a line of position on which the ship is. An example will make this clearer.

Suppose we take an altitude of the sun in the forenoon and find that it is 40°. Then the observed zenith distance is 50°, or 50 × 60 = 3000 miles. We therefore know that we must be somewhere on the circumference of a circle, the radius of which is 3000 miles, and the centre of which is the sub-solar point.

At the same time we find the true bearing to be (say) S. 45° E.

Now using our D.R. position and the hour angle and declination of the sun we can calculate what the zenith distance should be, by means of the spherical triangle.

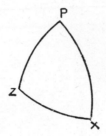

P is the pole.
Z is the D.R. position of the ship.
X is the sun, or sub-solar point.
$Z P X$ is the hour angle.
$Z X$ is the calculated zenith distance.

We will say that in this case the calculated zenith distance is 50° 10′, which means that we ought to be 3010 miles from the sun.

We assumed that we were at the D.R. position, but after taking the sight we found that we were in reality 10 miles nearer the sun in a direction S. 45° E. from the D.R. position. Therefore we are somewhere on the circumference of the inner circle. As this circle has a very large radius, the part of the circumference on which the ship is situated may be considered as a

straight line drawn at right angles to the true bearing
of the sun, and this line is called the Position Line.

We cannot plot the position of the sun and draw
this line at a distance of 3000 miles from it, but we can
plot the D.R. position on the chart and draw the position
line 10 miles from it, and this is what is done in practice.

From this one sight we do not know the actual position
of the ship, but we do know the position of the line on
which the ship is, and by means of a second sight later
on we can fix the ship's position.   Before considering the
question of this second sight we will find out how the
first position line is determined.

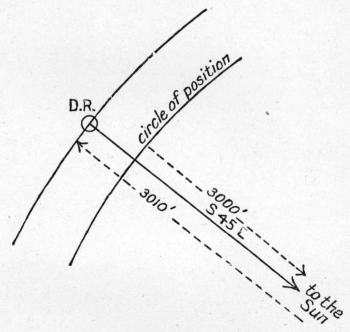

Let us see how the zenith distance from the D.R. position is calculated.

We know our D.R. latitude, and hence we know PZ the co-latitude. We also know the G.M.T. and the D.R. longitude, and from these we can get the S.M.T. and by applying E to it we find the hour angle. (In this case the angle ZPX will be the easterly hour angle.) Knowing the G.M.T., we can look up the declination of the sun, and hence we know the polar distance PX.

It will be seen, therefore, that in the spherical triangle we know the angle at P, and PZ and PX. We can calculate from these the zenith distance ZX.

The fundamental formula as given in Chapter V. was

$$\text{Hav } P = \frac{\text{hav } ZX - \text{hav } (PZ \sim PX)}{\text{sine } PZ \times \text{sine } PX}$$

Transposing so as to get ZX on the left hand side of the equation we have hav $ZX =$ hav $P \times$ sine $PZ \times$ sine $PX +$ hav $(PZ \sim PX)$.

Now it will be seen that PZ is $90° \pm$ Lat., and PX is $90° \pm$ Dec., and in order to save the trouble of this subtracting from or adding to $90°$, instead of taking the sine of $PZ \times$ sine of PX we change it into cosine of latitude $\times$ cosine of declination. (The reason for this is that the sine of $90° \pm$ an angle = the cosine of the angle.)

Also, instead of taking the difference between PZ and PX we add the latitude and declination if they have different names (one N. and the other S.), and subtract them if they have the same names. *S*ame names, *S*ubtract.

So our formula for practical purposes becomes hav $ZX =$ hav P cos lat. cos dec. $+$ hav (lat $\sim$ dec).

H

Example:

On January 4, 1933, at about 0930 ship time, in D.R. Lat. 30° 20′ N., Long. 40° 18′ W., the obs. alt. ☉ was 25° 10′ 30″ and the chronometer showed 12h 15m 30s, and was fast on G.M.T. 2m 15s; index error 2′ 30″+; height of eye 12 ft.; sun's true bearing S. 40° E. Calculate the zenith distance, then find the observed zenith distance and the position line.

R.S.T.	9h	30m	0s	Jan. 4
Long. W.	2	41	12	
G.D.	12	11	12	Jan. 4
Chron.	12	15	30	
Fast		2	15	
G.M.T.	12	13	15	Jan. 4
Long. W.	2	41	12	
S.M.T.	9	32	3	
E +	11	55	0	
H.A.	21	27	3	

$$\begin{cases} \text{Dec. S. } 22° 44\cdot6' \\ E \ 11\text{h } 55\text{m } 0\text{s} \end{cases}$$

This is the angle at *P* measured westwards. In order to look up its haversine we look along the bottom of the page for the hours and minutes, and up the right hand side for the seconds.

We now proceed to work out the formula to find *Z X*. As hav *P* cos lat. cos dec. are all multiplied together we look up the log hav and the log cos and add them. Then look up the natural haversine, and add to it the natural haversine of the lat∼dec.

H.A. 21h 27m 3s   log hav   9·03050 ⎫
Lat. 30° 20′ N.   log cos   9·93606 ⎬ Add
Dec. 22° 44·6 S.   log cos   9·96485 ⎭

L. +D. 53° 4·6′   log hav (2)   8·93141

nat hav   ·08539 ⎫
nat hav   ·19962 ⎭

nat hav of $Z\,X$ ·28501
$Z\,X$ or calculated zenith distance
= 64° 32′

Now find the observed zenith distance, which will be the true one.

Obs. alt.   25° 10·5′
I.E.   +   2·5

           25° 13·0′
Corr.   +   11·0

True alt.   25° 24′
           90

Obs. zen. dist.   64° 36′

Now if we subtract the calculated zenith distance from the observed zenith distance, the result will be the distance that the position line is from the D.R. position, and is called the Intercept.

As the observed zenith distance is greater than the calculated zenith distance, we must be further away from the sun than we thought we were according to the D.R. position, therefore the intercept is measured away from the D.R. along the true bearing.

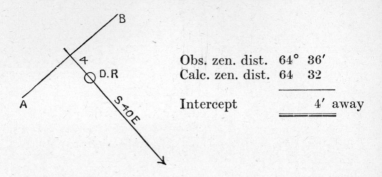

Obs. zen. dist. 64° 36'
Calc. zen. dist. 64   32

Intercept   4' away

Lay off the sun's true bearing S. 40° E. from the D.R. position, and produce it backwards. Mark off the intercept 4 miles and draw the position line *A B* at right angles.

We know now that the ship is somewhere on this line, and nothing more can be done until the sun's bearing has altered after a few hours.

Now suppose the ship in the meanwhile has remained in the same position. (Actually this would never happen, but it will be easier to understand.) At about

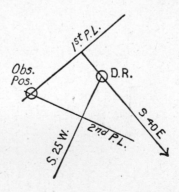

1·30 p.m. we take another sight, and work it out in exactly the same way. Let us suppose that the sun's true bearing is now S. 25° W., and the intercept is this time 5 miles nearer (*i.e.* the observed zenith distance is less than the calculated zenith distance).

From the same D.R. position we lay off the true bearing S. 25° W., and draw the position line at right angles to it, 5 miles towards the sun. The point at which the two position lines cut is the position of the ship (obs. pos.).

In actual practice the vessel would not have been stationary during the two sights, so let us see how the observed position is found assuming the speed to be 8 knots and the true course made good between 9·30 a.m. and 1·30 p.m., S. 70° W.

At 9·30 a.m. the sun's true bearing was S. 40° E. Intercept 4′ away.

At 1·30 p.m. the sun's true bearing was S. 25° W. Intercept 5′ nearer.

D.R. position at 9·30 was 30° 20′ N., 40° 18′ W.

The plotting may be done either on the chart or on squared paper—preferably the latter, because an ocean chart has a very small scale, whereas on squared paper it may be drawn as large as convenient.

First make a dot with a circle round it to mark the 9·30 D.R. position, and from it lay off the sun's T.B., S. 40° E., measuring the intercept 4 miles away, and draw the 1st position line. Now we know that the ship is *somewhere* on this, so we will assume that she is at *A*

For instance, suppose that at 6 p.m. in D.R. position Lat. 49° 40′ N., Long. 7° 15½′ W., the position line obtained by a sun sight passes through the D.R. in a direction N. 50° W., S. 50° E. (true). The ship's true course made good is east and speed 8 knots.

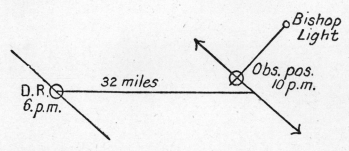

At 10 p.m. the Bishop Light bears N.E. (true).

Then by transferring the position line 32 miles along the course, and plotting the bearing of the Bishop Light the position of the ship at 10 p.m. will be the point where the two lines cut—namely 49° 44′ N., 6° 36′ W.

As in the case of terrestrial cross bearing the position will be found most accurately when the position line and the terrestrial bearing intersect at about 90° degrees.

CHAPTER VII.

AZIMUTHS.

In the position line example in Chapter VI. the true bearings of the sun were given, but it is not usual in practice to find the compass bearing and then correct it for deviation and variation, owing to the difficulty of taking a bearing of the sun accurately.

Within certain limits of latitude the true bearing may be found by means of Azimuth Tables (Burdwood's).

The azimuth of a celestial body is the angle between the meridian passing through the zenith and the great circle passing through the zenith and the body. In the figure the azimuth of X is the angle PZX, or roughly N. 130° E.

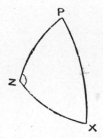

In the foregoing example, the first bearing S. 40° E. expressed as the azimuth would be N. 140° E., and the second azimuth would be N. 155° W.

In order to use the *Burdwood's Azimuth Tables* we

must know the latitude of the ship and the declination of the sun, to the nearest degree, and the apparent time at the ship.

To find the apparent time, if the hour angle is more than 12 hours subtract 12 hours from it, and the result will be the ship apparent time A.M.

If the hour angle is less than 12 hours it is the same as the ship apparent time P.M.

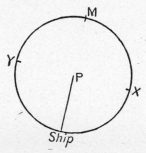

In the figure on the plane of the equator, when the sun is at *M* the hour angle is 12 hours and the apparent time is 0h (midnight).   When the sun is at *X* the hour angle is 18 hours, and the apparent time is 6 A.M.   When the sun is at *Y* the hour angle is 6 hours, and the apparent time is 6 P.M.

Referring to the example in the last chapter, the hour angle of the sun was 21h 27m 3s, so the apparent time was 9h 27m 3s A.M.

The D.R. latitude was 30° 20′ N. and the declination of the sun was S. 22° 44·6′.

In the Azimuth Tables at the top of the page we find latitude 30°, and as the latitude is North and the declination is South we take the page showing "Declination Contrary Name to Latitude." (See table at end of book.) Then under 23° declination, and opposite IXh 28m, on the left hand side, the azimuth is found to be 141° 3′. As the ship is in North latitude, and the apparent time is A.M. we read the azimuth from North to East, therefore in this case it is N. 141° E. By interpolating between latitude 30° and latitude 31°, and between declination 22° and 23° we can obtain the azimuth more accurately, but for practical purposes one degree is sufficiently correct.

The Azimuth Tables may also be used to find the azimuth of a star, but in this case the hour angle is used instead of apparent time. This will be explained later.

If no Azimuth Tables are available, or if the latitude of the ship is outside the limits of the tables, the azimuth must be calculated by means of the spherical triangle, or the bearing of the celestial body must be taken by compass and the variation and deviation applied to it.

The azimuth is calculated from the triangle by means of the fundamental formula in a similar way to the hour angle in the "Longitude by Chronometer" problem.

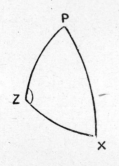

The azimuth is the angle at Z.
PZ is the co-latitude.
P X is the polar distance.
Z X is the zenith distance (observed).

Therefore as we know all three sides of the triangle we can find the angle Z by means of the formula hav $Z=$ {hav $P\,X$—hav $(Z\,P{\sim}Z\,X)$} cosec $Z\,P$ cosec $Z\,X$.

In the position line example on page 103 the declination was S. 22° 44·6′, therefore $P\,X=90°+22°\ 44\cdot6'=112°$ 44·6′.

The D.R. latitude was 30° 20′ N., therefore $Z\,P=90°-$ 30° 20′=59° 40′.

The observed zenith distance $Z\,X$ was 64° 36′. The observed zenith distance is used because it is more correct than the calculated.

$P\,X$	= 112°	44·6′	nat hav	·69329
$Z\,X$	= 64°	36′		
$Z\,P$	= 59°	40′		
$\sim$	= 4°	56′	nat hav	·00185
				·69144
			log hav	9·83976
$Z\,X$	= 64°	36′	log cosec	·04415
$Z\,P$	= 59°	40′	log cosec	·06394
			log hav Z	9·94785
			Z =	140° 41′

Therefore the calculated azimuth is N. 141° E. to the nearest degree, which is the same result as we obtained from the Azimuth Tables.

CHAPTER VIII.

STAR POSITION LINES.

THE position of the ship may be found by the Marcq St. Hilaire method by either simultaneous altitudes of two stars, or of one star and a planet, the mode of procedure being the same.

It will be remembered that in working a sun sight by the Marcq St. Hilaire method it was necessary to find the hour angle of the true sun, and the same applies to a star sight.

In the figure on the plane of the equator, the arc γZ is the right ascension of the meridian (R.A.M.), and this is always equal to the S.M.T. $+R$.

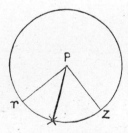

Now it will be seen that the arc $\gamma Z = \gamma X + Z X$. γX is the right ascension of the star X, and $Z X$ is its hour angle.

Therefore R.A.M.   = R.A. + H.A.
and S.M.T. $+ R$ = R.A. + H.A.
therefore H.A.   = S.M.T. $+ R$ − R.A.

and as S.M.T. = G.M.T. ± longitude, the formula becomes
H.A. of star = G.M.T. ± long. + *R* − R.A. of star.

In the following example we will find the position of
the ship by the nearly simultaneous altitudes of two
stars.

Example.—At about 0530 at ship, on January 5,
1933, in D.R. position Lat. 30° 10′ S., Long. 15° W.,
the observed altitude of Regulus was 34° 52′ 10″; G.M.T.
6h 33m 20s. Also the obs. alt. of Antares was 39° 15′
24″; G.M.T. 6h 35m 10s; height of eye 12 ft.; index
error 2′ 30″ +.

G.M.T.		6h 33m 20s	Jan. 5 *R* = 6h 57m 37s		
Long. W.	1	0 0	Dec. Regulus N.12° 17·6′		
			R.A. ,, 10h 4m 50s		
S.M.T.		5 33 20			
R	+	6 57 37			
R.A.M.		12 30 57			
R.A.	−	10 4 50			
H.A.		2h 26m 7s	log hav	8·99221
Lat.		30° 10′ S.	log cos	9·93680
Dec		12° 17·6′ N.	log cos	9·98992
L + D		42° 27·6′	log hav	8·91893
			nat hav	·08298
			nat hav	
		L + D		·13113

nat hav zen. dist.   ·21411

calculated zen. dist.   55° 7·5′

Obs. alt. Regulus 34° 52·2'
I.E.   +   2·5
                  ─────────────
                  34   54·7
Star corr.   —   4·8
                  ─────────────
True alt.   34   49·9
                    90
                  ─────────────
Obs. zen. dist.   55° 10·1'
Calc. zen. dist.   55°   7·5'
                  ─────────────
Intercept away   2·6'
                  ═════════════

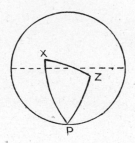

Before we can draw the position line, the azimuth of Regulus must be found, namely the angle *P Z X*, and the Sun Azimuth Tables can be used for this, as the latitude of the ship is between 30° and 60°.

Instead of using apparent time we use the hour angle of Regulus, which is 2h 26m (to the nearest minute), the angle *Z P X* in the figure. As it is less than 12 hours it corresponds to apparent time P.M.

Now with Lat. 30° on the page showing "Declination Contrary Name to Latitude," in the column 12° declination and opposite "Apparent Time P.M." 2h 26m (that is between 24 and 28) we find that the azimuth of Regulus is 134½°. As we are in South latitude and the hour angle is less than 12h westward, the azimuth is from south to west—S. 134½° W. If the latitude of the ship had not been between the limits 30°—60° North or South, or if the declination of the star had been greater than 23°, the azimuth could not have been found by Burdwood's Tables.

However, Goodwin's *Azimuth Tables for the Higher Declinations* are tabulated between 0° and 60° for latitude, and 24° and 30° for declination, and these can be used for all planet sights and many of the conspicuous stars. If the azimuth cannot be found by either of the tables, it should be calculated by means of the formula in exactly the same way as for the azimuth of the sun.

The second sight (Antares) is now worked in a similar manner.

G.M.T.	6h 35m 10s	Jan. 5	$R =$ 6h 57m 37s
Long. W.	1 0 0		Dec Antares S. 26° 17·2′
			R.A. „ 16h 25m 17s
S.M.T.	5 35 10		
$R \ +$	6 57 37		
R.A.M.	12 32 47		Add 24 hours in order to
R.A. —	16 25 17		subtract the R.A.
H.A.	20h 7m 30s.	log hav	9·37285*
Lat.	30° 10′ S.	log cos	9·93680
Dec.	26° 17·2′ S.	log cos	9·95260
$L - D$	3° 52·8′	log hav	9·26225
		nat hav	·18292
	nat hav $L - D$		·00115
	nat hav zen. dist.		·18407
	calc. zen. dist.		50° 48·7′

* The hour angle will be found at the bottom of the Haversine Table.

Note.—As the declination and latitude have the same names they are subtracted.

Obs. alt. Antares	39°	15·4′
I.E. +		2·5′
	39	17·9
Star corr. —		4·6
True alt	39	13·3
	90	
Obs. zen. dist.	50°	46·7′
Calc. zen. dist.	— 50°	48·7′
Intercept nearer	2 miles.	

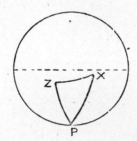

In this case, the declination being greater than 23°, the azimuth must either be found from Goodwin's Tables or calculated as follows.

In the triangle $P\,Z\,X$, $P\,X = 90° - 26°\ 17\cdot2' = 63°\ 42\cdot8'$

$$Z\,X = 50°\quad 46\cdot7'$$

$$Z\,P = 90° - 30°\ 10' = 59°\ 50'$$

The fundamental haversine formula to find the angle Z

I

is hav $Z = \{$hav $PX -$ hav $(ZX \sim ZP)\}$ cosec ZX cosec ZP.

PX	63°	42·8′	nat hav	·27857
ZP	59°	50′		
ZX	50°	46·7′		
$\sim$	9°	3·3′	nat hav	·00623
				·27234

			log hav	9·43511
ZX	50°	46·7′	log cosec	0·11087
ZP	59°	50′	log cosec	0·06320
			log hav Z	9·60918
		$Z =$		79° 14′

As the hour angle (measured westwards from the ship's meridian) is about 20 hours, the easterly hour angle is about 4 hours, and therefore the star is to the east of the ship, and the azimuth is S. 79° E.

Now collecting the results of the two sights we can plot the position lines on squared paper, and hence find the observed position of the ship.

> *Regulus* Azimuth S. $134\frac{1}{2}$° W.
> True bearing N. $45\frac{1}{2}$° W.
> Intercept 2·6 miles away.

> *Antares* Azimuth (and true bearing) S. 79° E.
> Intercept 2 miles nearer.

First plot the position of the D.R. and lay off the true bearing of Regulus N. $45\frac{1}{2}$° W. and produce it backwards. Measure off the intercept of 2·6 miles from the D.R. away from the direction of the star, using one large square to represent one mile. Draw the position line at right angles to the bearing.

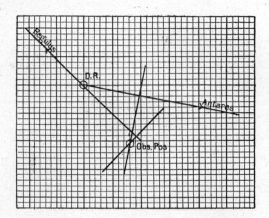

Then lay off the true bearing of Antares S. 79° E. from the D.R. and measure off the intercept of 2 miles towards the star. Draw the position line at right angles to the bearing.

The point at which the two position lines cut is the position of the ship at the time of the sights.

To find the latitude and longitude of this position, measure the vertical distance between the D.R. and the observed position. This is 2·1′ and is the difference of latitude south.

The D.R. latitude was	30°	10′ S.
D. lat		2·1 S.
Observed lat.	30°	12·1′ S.

Now measure the horizontal distance between the D.R. and the observed position. This is 1·6′ and is the departure east.

Look in the "Departure into D. longitude" Table with 30° as middle latitude and 16 as departure, and in the difference of longitude column will be found 18·5′. Therefore as the departure was actually 1·6 instead of 16 the difference of longitude will be 1·85′ east.

The D.R. long. was	15°	0′ W.
D. long.		1·8′ E.
Observed long.	14°	58·2′ W.

The observed position of the ship was therefore Lat. 30° 12·1′ S., Long. 14° 58·2′ W.

A planet sight is worked in exactly the same way as a star sight, but, owing to the planets being much nearer the earth than the stars, their declinations and right ascensions vary much more rapidly, and they will be found in the *Nautical Almanac* tabulated for every day in the year instead of once a month as in the case of the stars.

CHAPTER IX.

LATITUDE BY EX-MERIDIAN ALTITUDE.

ON a cloudy day when the sun only appears occasionally it may not be possible to obtain an altitude at noon, but if it appears a short time before or after, preferably within half an hour of noon, the latitude may still be found quite easily. The latitude obtained will, however, be the latitude at the time of the sight and not at noon.

Let us suppose that we are able to take an altitude of the sun 25 minutes before it reaches the meridian.

In the figure, *P* is the North pole, *E R* is the equator, *Z* is the position of the ship, *X* is the sub-solar point, *D C* is the circle of declination, and *Z P X* is the easterly hour angle of the sun, in this case 25 minutes.

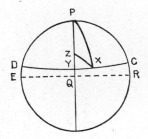

Now the latitude at the time of taking the sight is *Z Q*, and this is equal to *Z Y* +*Y Q*.

Z Y is the meridian zenith distance, and *Y Q* is the declination. The problem is therefore to find *Z Y*.

121

The sun's altitude when on the meridian is greater than at any other time, provided the ship is not travelling fast in a northerly or southerly direction, and consequently the meridian zenith distance must be least, except in very high latitudes when the sun might be below the pole. Therefore $Z\,Y$ must be less than $Z\,X$, the observed zenith distance. The difference between $Z\,X$ and ZY can be found by means of the Ex-Meridian Tables in Inman's.

As the zenith distance$=90°$—altitude, or the altitude $=90°$—zenith distance, this correction (*i.e* the difference between $Z\,X$ and $Z\,Y$) may be either subtracted from the observed zenith distance $Z\,X$, or added to the observed altitude. The latter is usually done.

Example.—On Jan. 6, 1933, in D.R. Lat. 41° 46′ N., Long. 33° 26′ W., the obs alt ☉ near the meridian was 25° 16′ south of the observer; height of eye 12 ft.; the G.M.T. by chron. was 13h 52m 33s (Jan 6). Find the latitude at the time of the observation.

In order to use Ex-Meridian Table No. 1 in Inman's we must know the rough latitude and declination to the nearest degree. If the latitude is bigger than the declination we look it up in the left hand column and the declination along the top, and *vice versa*.

To use Table 2 we need the hour angle (the E.H.A. if before noon) therefore we must know E in order to *add* it to the S.M.T.

H.A. $-E=$S.M.T., therefore H.A.$=$S.M.T.$+E$.

```
G.M.T.        13h 52m 33s (Jan. 6) {Dec =S. 22° 30·6'
Long. W.       2  13  44           {E  = 11h 54m 5s

S.M.T.        11  38  49
E     +       11  54   5

Hour angle    23  32  54

E.H.A.         0h 27m  6s
```

Now correct the observed altitude for height of eye, etc.

```
Obs. alt.      25° 16'
Sun's corr.  +     11'

True alt.      25° 27'
```

Turn to Table 1, and with Lat. 42° and Dec. 22½° (we must interpolate between 22 and 23) on the page which has CONTRARY names on it, because the latitude is N. and the declination is S., we find 9·882. Turn to Table 2, and with hour angle 27m 6s we find 7·543.

These two logarithms must be added together.

```
9·882
7·543

17·425 or 7·425
```

Turn to Table 3, and look in the faint type for 7·425 and it will be found that the correction to be *added* to the altitude is 18·3'.

(If this correction has been a large one it would have been necessary to apply a second correction to it from Table 4.)

True alt.	25°	27′	
Ex.-meridian corr. +		18·3	
Meridian alt.	25	45·3	South of observer
	90		
Meridian zen. dist.	64	14·7	
Declination	22	30·6	South
Latitude at sights	41°	44·1′	North

The latitude may be found in the same way if the sun has crossed the meridian, the only difference being that the hour angle must not be subtracted from 24 hours. The ex-meridian correction is still added to the true altitude.

It may happen that when the altitude has been taken it is found to be outside the scope of the tables, and if this is the case the sight should be worked in the ordinary way by the Marcq St. Hilaire method, which will give the position line. As the true bearing of the sun will not be south or north, the position line will not be parallel with the equator, and consequently will not give the true latitude.

However the ship will be somewhere on this line, and if a longitude sight has been worked the two together will give the position.

————

The chief difficulty experienced in taking accurate sights, especially in small craft, is due to uncertainty in the position of the horizon.

In a heavy sea the height of eye will vary considerably,

and hence the value of the dip will also vary, as may be seen by referring to the Table of Dip of Sea Horizon in the Nautical Tables. In small vessels where the height of eye is normally about 10 ft., the dip may vary by several minutes, which produces an error in position of several miles.

Another source of error is due to abnormal refraction near the sea. If there is a considerable difference between the temperatures of the sea and air, the refraction or bending of the rays of light will be greater than usual, and in consequence the visible horizon may be further away, thus altering the dip.

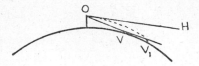

In the figure, an observer at O would see the horizon at V if there were no refraction, but if the temperatures of the sea and air were different the visible horizon would be at V_1, and the direction of the horizon would be along the tangent to the curve, namely OH.

A correction table for abnormal refraction is given in the Nautical Tables, but is very seldom used in yachts.

However, in a moderate sea, altitude can be taken with quite a fair degree of accuracy, especially in the case of meridian altitudes of the sun. The writer has on several occasions worked a latitude sight correct to within half a mile when in an 18-ft. boat in a moderate sea.

When taking the altitude of a body when off the

meridian, such as a longitude by chronometer or Marcq St. Hilaire sight, it is best to take three altitudes in as short an interval as possible, and then take the mean of the altitudes and the mean of the times.

The best time to take the altitude is when it is changing rapidly, but when this occurs the body will often be near the horizon, and consequently the error due to uncertainty in the amount of refraction will be great. Therefore whenever possible the altitude should be taken when the body is near the prime vertical so long as the latitude and declination have the same names, because in this case the altitude will be rapidly changing but the body will be well above the horizon.

In a yacht or any small craft a chronometer watch or deck watch is preferable to a chronometer, as the quick violent motion is not so liable to affect the smaller instrument. It should always be wound at the same time every day, so that its rate will be as constant as possible.

When taking a sight the upper part of the body should be free to move in any direction, and although it may often be necessary to wedge oneself firmly into a corner, the hand should never be used to hold on to a shroud, as this will make the upper part of the body too rigid.

CHAPTER X.

DEVIATION BY AMPLITUDE.

I⊤ is sometimes necessary to check the deviation of the compass at sea, because in heavy weather it is liable to change.

The deviation may be found during the day by the sun, and at night by the pole star if this is visible.

The simplest method is by finding the true amplitude of the sun.

When the sun's declination is north it always rises to the north of east and sets to the north of west, and similarly when the declination of the sun (or any other body) is south it rises to the south of east and sets to the south of west.

The angle between the body when rising (or setting) and the east (or west) point is called the bearing amplitude, and is named from the east or west points towards the north or south. Thus if the sun's true bearing when rising is N. 70° E. its bearing amplitude is E. 20° N., and if the true bearing at sunset is S. 65° W. the amplitude is W. 25° S.

The amplitude of a celestial body may be found from a table in Inman's, and all that is required is the latitude of the ship and the declination of the body to the nearest degree. Under each degree of declination two columns will be seen, but it is only the one showing bearing amplitude that we need for finding the deviation.

The procedure is as follows:—The declination of the sun (or other body) is ascertained from the *Nautical Almanac*, and using this and the latitude of the ship the true amplitude is found from the table and is named accordingly as the sun is rising or setting.

The compass bearing of the sun is taken at the time of true rising or setting, and this will not be when the sun's lower limb is on the horizon. The actual time of rising or setting is when the sun's centre is on the rational horizon, and owing to refraction this will be when the sun's lower limb appears to be at a distance above the visible horizon equal to its semi-diameter—that is when

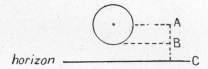

$BC=AB$. We now have the true amplitude and the observed (or compass) amplitude, and the difference between these will be the compass error. By applying the variation, as ascertained from the chart, the deviation will be found. It will, of course, only have this value when the ship is on the same course.

Example.—While steering a certain course in Lat. 51° N., Long. 6° W. on Jan. 2, 1933, the sun was observed to bear by compass S. 31° E. on rising.

Find the deviation of the compass, the variation being 15° 21′ W.

On Jan. 2, the declination is S. 23° to the nearest

degree, and with Latitude 51° we find that the bearing
amplitude is 38·4°.   As the sun is rising and the declination is south the amplitude must be E. 38° S. which
means that the sun's true bearing is S. 51·6° E.   By
subtracting the compass bearing from it we find the
compass error, and applying the variation to this gives
the deviation.

Sun's true bearing	S.	51°	36′ E.
Sun's compass bearing	S.	31°	0′ E.
Compass error		20°	36′ W.
Variation		15°	21′ W.
Deviation		5°	15′ W.

The deviation may also be found by taking a compass
bearing of the sun and noting the time.   Then from this
the apparent time at the ship is calculated, and the
sun's true bearing found from the Azimuth Tables.
The procedure is then the same as in the latter part of the
foregoing example.